CITY OF NATIONS

The Evolution of New York City's Multiculturalism

AF139574

A historical view on New York's immigrants

by

Eva Kolb

&

Textwerkstatt München

**To my family
&
the city which has stolen
my heart**

This book is a new edition of the book "The Evolution of New York City's Multiculturalism: Melting Pot or Salad Bowl: Immigrants in New York from the 19th Century until the End of the Gilded Age".

Cover: Statue of Liberty from below, front.
Photo shot by Derek Jensen (Tysto), 2004-September-26

List of Contents

שפּײז וועט געווינעז דיא קריעג!

אידר קומט אהער צו געפינעז פרייהייט.

יעצט מוזט אידר העלפֿעז זיא צו בעשיצעז

מיר מוזעז דיא עלליעס פֿערזארגעז מיט ווייץ.

לאזט קייז זאד ניט גייז איז ניווערץ

יוניטעד סטייטס שפּײז פֿערוואלטונג.

United States Food Administration color lithograph World War I poster by Charles Edward Chambers (1883-1941), showing immigrants arriving in New York harbor. Caption (translated from the yiddish): "Food will win the war. You came here seeking freedom, now you must help to preserve it. Wheat is needed for the allies. Waste nothing." Charles Edward Chambers (illustrator). Rusling Wood, Litho., New York (publisher), 1917

"Give me your tired, your poor,
Your huddled masses yearning to
breathe free,
The wretched refuse of your teeming
shore.
Send these, the homeless, tempest-
tost to me,
I lift my lamp beside the golden
door!"
(Emma Lazarus, 1883, final stanza of
her poem about the Statue of
Liberty: 'The New Colossus')

2007 Presidential $1 Coin image from the United States Mint

Introduction

This book deals with the formation of New York City's multicultural character during the 19th century until the end of the third decade of the 20th century. It draws a sketch of the metropolis' first big immigration waves and describes the development of immigrants who entered the New World as foreigners and strangers and soon became one of the most essential parts of the city's very character.

A main focus is laid upon the ambiguity of the immigrants' identity which is captured between assimilation and separation. One of the most important questions the book deals with is, whether the city can be seen as one of the world's greatest melting pots or just as a huge salad bowl inhabiting all kinds of different cultures. The book approaches these topics from an historical and a fictional point of view and concentrates on personal experiences of the immigrants as well as on the cultural impact these immigration waves had on the megalopolis New York.

During the first chapter the book summarizes the historical development of immigration in New York and gives a short overall view on the topic. Chapter II deals with the journey and the arrival of the immigrants in the New World. This part of the book takes a look at the hopes, fears and disappointments which accompanied the newcomers. It also gives a description of the famous immigration station Ellis Island.

The third chapter examines the living and working conditions of the early immigrants. It draws a sketch of some of the notorious districts, illustrates life inside the tenement buildings and reports about sweatshops and settlement houses. Besides, this chapter refers to the improvements made by organizations and social reformers. The third chapter also takes a look into the present to draw a parallel between the lives of the early and contemporary immigrants.

Chapter IV informs about the evolution of several ethnic districts of the city. Some of these quarters like "Kleindeutschland" or "Jewtown" are described in detail. It is mentioned what life in the several districts was like and why the immigrants started to create these miniaturized replicas of their mother countries. Furthermore, one can read about the immigrants' movements within the city over the decades and centuries.

The fifth chapter deals with the ambiguity of the immigrants' identity and therefore with the book's main thesis. This part investigates the often twofold kind of life which was lived especially by the first generation immigrants. The question arises, if New York City is a perfect example of the melting pot or just another salad bowl, or if none of these two characterizations defines the city's soul.

The book wants to show that the metropolis is a unique example of multicultural urban life. It's a place where melting pot and salad bowl exist next to each other, a city where amalgamation and separation, tight and vast social structures, old and new values, modern and antique styles and attitudes live together and manage to harmonize.

City of Nations displays a variety of visual impressions of the early immigrants. These pictures help to imagine their living and working conditions.

Since there were a huge number of writers, a couple of them very famous, others rather unknown, among the early immigrants, this book approaches its topics and main thesis with the help of several fictional texts.

Some of these novels and stories discussed in this book are *Bread Givers, Hungry Hearts & Other Stories, Red Ribbon on a White Horse, Salome of the Tenements* and *How I Found America* by Anzia Yezierska, *Yekl* and *The Rise of David Levinsky* by Abraham Cahan, *Manhattan Transfer* by John Dos Passos, and others.

Redraft of the Castello Plan New Amsterdam in 1660. John Wolcott Adams (1874–1925) and I.N. Phelps Stokes (1867–1944), drawn in 1916

I.   A Historical Summary

The "American society may be visualized as a cluster of immigrant-ethnic communities lapped by an expanding core population of mixed origins and indeterminate size" (Higham, 1998, p.13).

The Unites States have not received the most immigrants worldwide; Argentina or Brazil, for example, became the home of much more aliens. But there was certainly no other nation which had incomers originating from such a variety of countries and cultures, especially in New York.

New York has always been a colorful city of different nations united under the roof of one single city. When the Dutch founded New Amsterdam in 1625, after they had bought the island from the Indians for trinkets, it took less than twenty years until 18 diverse languages were spoken in the colonial town. In 1643 the Dutch colony had already gained its multicultural and multiethnic character which it should never ever lose again throughout its almost 400 years of history and its development from a Dutch, over a British colony up to an independent American city.

The first immigrants, though involuntary, arrived in 1626 and were slaves, imported from Angola. These African-Americans arrived in the New World long before any Jews or Roman Catholics inhabited the city. Even though they had to live under brutal and cruel conditions, they managed to survive. And in 1644 there was already the first free black community which consisted of 11 people who were given a piece of land they could cultivate. However, this right of possessing own ground was revoked from the free black people in 1716, after some slaves had started a revolt.

In New York slaves used to be domestic servants or artisans. During the long time of slavery, resistance occurred almost every day and often it found a violent end. The ways rebellious slaves were killed exceeds all imagination. Historical documents describe the burning of one slave "over slow fire for eight to ten hours" (Homberger, 1998, p.44).

During their supremacy, the Dutch always had the commanding position in the New Netherland society – at no time it was one of their immigrants. And even when the British took over power in 1664 and turned New Amsterdam into New York, the Dutch remained the dominant group among the settlers for the first 20 years. This was due to the fact that there were just a few English, Irish and Scottish families who emigrated to New York during that time.

However, the internationality of the city had already found its beginning during the Dutch reign, with the first schoolmaster of the city being a French immigrant who came to New Amsterdam in 1637, with all public documents being issued in English, Dutch and French between 1648-58 and with the fact that town proclamations were bilingual, namely Dutch and French since 1656. As a consequence the French Church was founded in the Dutch colonial town in 1659.

The first Jews, respectively Sephardic Jews who came from Portugal and Spain, arrived in New Amsterdam in 1654. They had to flee from their former asylum home Pernambuco over Curacao when the Portuguese re-conquered the Brazilian city. At first Peter Stuyvesant, the last Dutch Director-General of the colony of New Netherland, and his Council were against the immigration of Jews to the city. However they finally had to accept them since the Dutch West India Company was supported by a considerable number of Jewish investors. This small amount of 27 Jews was finally allowed to stay and after a while they got the opportunity to possess real estate, gain a foothold in trade and eventually became citizens of the city with all burgher rights.

Since the 1680s, when more and more people came to the U.S. to search for political and religious freedom, the process of immigration had found its beginning. Although there were several immigration restriction laws, wars and economic crises which helped to reduce the numbers of new arrivals drastically from time to time.

After 1685 more and more Jews and French Huguenots arrived in New York. Together with the British they soon became the commercial elite of the city. The Huguenots who survived the bloody massacre of Saint Bartholomew's Day in 1572, had been protected for more than one hundred years with the so-called Edict of Nantes which was formulated by Henri IV. However, in 1685 the revocation of the Edict forced about 200,000 Huguenots to emigrate to other countries. They moved to England, the Netherlands, Germany and of course, however in small groups at first, to the colonies in America.

Under the British supremacy prosperous times started, especially for the Jews. Jewish burial grounds, the first

Hebrew School as well as the first synagogue were established within the city's borders between 1682 and 1730. With the growing cosmopolitan character of New York, the Dutch language also could not persist in the long run. According to the diversity of churches situated on the tip of Manhattan Island by the middle of the 18th century, one could already recognize the manifold cultural, ethnic and religious appearance of New York.

The immigrants and the ideology they brought to their new home country, helped the Americans to clearly separate from their former British mother country. This was absolutely essential for their argumentation towards independence from England.

Already in the 18th century one could describe the Americans as a cosmopolitan people. These were the first steps towards the multinational city of New York as it is known today. However, vast multiculturalism with its tremendous multi-ethnic character and its colorful appearance which will find no equivalence all over the world was shaped a good deal later, when the masses from abroad streamed into the metropolis and formed the whole city structure totally new.

After the American Revolution and the War of Independence the British colonial town New York turned into an American city, inhabiting 12,000 people by 1783.

At the time of the city's rebuilding there were still a couple of thousand slaves. Only a small number of about 1,000 blacks were free at that time. However, the "Gradual Manumission Act" of 1799 freed all children of slaves who were born after July 4th of the same year. Already in 1810 the city of New York had the largest amount of free blacks in the whole country and in 1820 there were only a little more than 500 slaves living in the metropolis. By 1827 all slaves were freed finally.

By the end of the 18th century inhabitants with a Dutch background were becoming less in proportion. Despite the Germans who populated the city with some thousand people, the Irish with about 5,000 souls became one of the largest and fastest growing groups of immigrants after the English.

The Irish were also the first big group of immigrants who had to experience the harsh urban conditions of the city which later became so symptomatic of life in a metropolis: "Poverty, overcrowded housing conditions, political prejudice, religious discrimination. Irish immigrants were living in conditions which made them particularly susceptible to the yellow fever epidemics which spread through the overcrowded city. A majority of the victims of the 1795 epidemic in New York were from Ireland" (Homberger, 1998, p.56).

Only in the 19th and 20th century, when immigration took on gigantic and sometimes even alarming dimensions one could recognize that the former Dutch and British colony was transformed into an international metropolis, an immigration megalopolis.

With the beginning of the 19th century immigration started on a large scale and soon the city turned into a colorful pot full of contrasts. The paradoxical face of the megalopolis showed wealthy and golden streets or even whole districts, where old aristocratic families and self-made men strolled down Fifth Avenue, surrounded by splendid mansions and stores designed with marble and magnificent decoration. However, it also displayed the foul and rotten areas of the city, where the poor population of New York City was at home. These poor quarters were crowded with people who were mostly immigrants hoping for the American Dream. A dream which was reflected in the personal immigrant success story, a few of them could actually tell. People like the merchant A.T. Stewart who was an orphan born in Belfast, Ireland and who immigrated to New York in 1818, or Madame Restell represented this desired ideal since they both finally ran their own successful businesses and owned a luxurious mansion on Fifth Avenue.

Within 30 years during the first half of the 19th century, the population of New York grew from 200,000 people to nearly one million inhabitants. Most of them started out in the slums and tenement districts of the metropolis. In his book *The Historical Atlas of New York City,* Eric Homberger gives a definition of this city of extreme contrasts in the 19th century:

> The notorious Old Brewery at Five Points and A.T. Stewart's Fifth Avenue mansion establish the extremes of a pervasive, simultaneous sense of opposite social, economic, and moral orders which defined the character of New York. Contrasts were legion: consider the magnificent commercial palace of Lord & Taylor on Broadway, and the cheap clothing shops on the Bowery; the elegant brownstone row houses above Washington Square which lined lower Fifth Avenue and the overcrowded, dilapidated structures on Delancey, Rivington, and Stanton Streets which housed the Irish immigrants. During

the day, Broadway was the home of the fashionable and elegant, at night it was haunted by prostitutes, con-men, and criminals. [...] Fifth Avenue was as much a complex symbol of the new spirit of the age of "go ahead" as were the notorious slums of Five Points. (Homberger, 1998, p.74/75)

There are a lot of myths and partial truths concerning the interpretation of immigration or immigrants' status on the whole. "One legend puts the immigrant, and all he represents, at the center of American experience. Another relegates him to the periphery" (Higham, 1984, p.4).

Maldwyn Jones writes in *A Nation of Immigrants* (1964) that immigration is "America's historic *raison d'être*... the most persistent and most pervasive influence in her development" (in Higham, 1984, p.4).

To a certain extent one can say that immigration plays one of the most important roles in the whole history of American life. American ideals like mobility, success stories or the American Dream result from the immigrant character of the nation.

Despite that, displacement describes an essential part in an American's experience. There exists a certain memory of being displaced from somewhere else which turns migration into a possible key to the character of the Americans.

Since the United States cannot look back on a deeply rooted national tradition, they believe in the future. This orientation towards a time to come has brought along American traits like "idealism; flexibility and adaptability to change; a dependence on the self and the immediate family more than the wider community; a high respect for personal achievement; a tendency to conform to the values of peers and neighbors instead of holding stubbornly to ancestral ways" (Higham, 1998, p.5). The immigrant built and builds America. However, the problem of separation and segregation had always been present in the history of the incomer.

The term immigrant occurred for the first time by the end of the 18th century. Only in 1789 the English language entitled newcomers with "immigrants" which was a result of a change in attitude. By then the new arrivals were rather identified with their new country of choice than with their former home country. This meant that there already had to be a nation and society in existence to which these people could choose to come. Therefore the term immigrant, which replaced the word emigrant, does not refer to the colonists or settlers who founded the nation and created the basis for everyone else to live there. More or less the immigrant can be described as someone who brings along a foreign culture to another nation.

The English who ruled huge parts of the country until the American Revolution and War of Independence, regarded themselves as founders of the nation. They laid the foundation of the cities, towns, laws, work, language and a lot of mental customs which had to be accepted and adopted by the immigrants.

However, this is also just part of the truth since one mustn't forget the Dutch who also founded important cities like New York, the Native Americans who had already established in this country, and those who arrived at the same time with the Dutch and British, but were certainly unwilling to come, like the slaves from Africa and the West Indies. Especially the slaves collide with "the great American success story"[1]

---

[1] Higham, John. *Send These to Me – Immigrants in Urban America*. 1998. p.6

which takes it for granted that the immigrants choose the U.S. for specific and voluntary reasons.

The internationality of America has its roots in the history of the nation's foundation. The American society established by incorporating a colorful group of diverse nationalities and ethnic groups through "invasion and conquest, by enslavement, and by immigration" (Higham, 1998, p.8). However, with the Anglo-Saxon majority maintaining the political control and power over the whole country "those who lose close contact with their immigrant origins are assimilated into a partially de-ethnicized host society" (Higham, 1998, p.11).

Optimally the ideal of the melting pot can be realized in the second generation of immigrants, with the children of immigrants and often due to international relationships and inter-ethnic marriage. But the success of a total assimilation is not guaranteed since the ethnic identity often remains alive within the larger background of families or ethnic districts.

An ethnic consciousness is likely to come up, letting the immigrants become assimilated Americans on the one hand, but making them proud of their own cultural heritage, their customs, traditions and overall identity on the other hand. The ethnic bond and background plays a huge role for many people in finding their identity or being integrated in a larger group of people with the same origins.

Certain values remain vivid in the cultural consciousness or way of living of immigrants, their children and the generations after them.

However, one also has to be aware of the differences between the diverse ethnic groups and the various generations. In the second or sometimes third generation many immigrants are likely to neglect their cultural and ethnic background and try to get fully Americanized without sticking to the old values and traditions. Yet, the generations afterwards often discover a new consciousness for their origins, and sometimes they even identify much more with their ethnic group than with their American nationality.

Intermarriage, however, complicates the search for identity since the intermingling with other cultures and races makes it almost impossible to clearly define one's roots after two or more generations.

Furthermore, one has to mention that some ethnic groups like the Jews are more likely to fully assimilate, while others, like the Hispanics or Chinese for example, tend to stay rather poly-cultural over the years. This is especially due to their districts as well as their outer appearance which always reminds them of their cultural and national background.

However, the presence of two different cultural nations within an immigrant's way of thinking and living sometimes ends up in a paradox with both identities fighting each other. So occasionally, people with a strong ethnic background may have problems in identifying with their origins as well as their adapted American way of life since both cultures are present within their souls. An immigrant might have learned to assimilate to the American way of life and cannot sympathize with his or her old traditions and values anymore; however, when it comes to politics, for example, he often strongly encourages those who belong to his ethnic background.

Joshua Fishman puts it this way: "To exist and yet not to exit, to be needed and yet to be unimportant, to be different and yet to be the same, to be integrated and yet to be separate" (Joshua A. Fishman, 1966 in Higham, 1998, p. 12).

Above: Castle Garden immigrant depot in New York City.

Below: Immigrants entering the United States through Ellis Island, the main
immigrant entry facility of the United States from 1892 to 1954. Picture taken in
1902.

Both pictures published on Wikimedia Commons, photographer unknown.

II.   Ellis Island: „Island of Hope, Island of Tears"

In the early 19th century masses of Irish who suffered from hunger and other problems in their home country came to America to start a new living. By the 1830s almost half of Ireland's population had left the green isle.

Besides, a huge immigration wave from Germany arrived approximately at the same time, when many hundreds of thousands Germans left their country due to the Revolution of 1848. They were the so-called Forty-Eighters.

Later on people arrived in masses. The biggest immigration wave arrived in the late 19th and early 20th century when mostly Eastern European Jews and Italians came to New York.

They left Europe and their familiar environment in groups, families and even whole villages. Very often they were also completely alone. Most of their belongings remained in their home country. Usually they sold it to friends and neighbors. Huge bundles stuffed with their most beloved items were the only things they brought to the New World. Generally it were only clothes and some little memories of their home country, sometimes just typical food which reminded them of the smell and flavor of their past. However, a lot of the immigrants tried to bring along as much as they could carry, even taking furniture to America. Others had almost nothing apart from their ticket for a fortnight's voyage as a steerage passenger on an overcrowded ship, the notorious $25 which they were supposed to show to the Ellis Island officers to prove that they had enough money to make a start, and some bread, sugar or fruits.

And so they left their home and started a long and exhausting journey, often through their whole country or sometimes even across Europe which took them several days and in some cases even weeks.

The persecuted among them, for example those who fled the pogroms in Russia which had cost the lives of many Jews, usually escaped in the shelter of the night, with their enemies right behind them. Mary Antin, a Jewish immigrant from Russia described the journey to the harbor of Hamburg with the following words: "Emigrants were herded at stations, packed in cars, and driven from place to place like cattle" (in Foner, 2000, p.29).

By foot, with ox-carts and trains the emigrants arrived at the big ports of Europe where they were inspected, checked and received their papers for the trip. Often they had to wait for a couple of days and sometimes even weeks until they were crowded on the ships which brought them to the Promised Land. In the meantime they had to sleep in dirty sticky rooms where only one third of the emigrants could find a place to sleep or eat.

Here at the ports much more people were sent back home than on Ellis Island. The inspections and investigations were strict and rough since the journey from America back to Europe had to be paid by the European shipyards themselves.

On the ships conditions were even worse than in the harbors. Squeezed in sticky, dark and crowded compartments that lacked any kind of hygiene and eating foul and old food, the passengers had to endure about two long weeks until they finally arrived in the New World.

Often there was only one toilet for 50 passengers and usually the ship was only cleaned on the day of arrival in New York to satisfy the commissioners who inspected them. There are even examples of ships where one fourth or fifth of the passengers died on the journey due to epidemics like cholera that broke out because of the horrible conditions. Some of the passengers on the ships cried so much during the trip that they were suspected to have trachoma when they were inspected on Ellis Island.

The first and second class passengers were treated with a lot of privileges. They were even allowed to leave the ship relatively soon after the arrival in New York. The steerage travelers were all brought to Ellis Island for further inspection. Their journey had not found an end yet. However, those who were prohibited to enter the country represented just a very small percentage of the whole bunch.

Having to watch the upper classes leaving without any kind of inspection often left a negative impression on the immigrants' minds. America's freedom and equality had some similarities with the class society back in Europe. The passengers had to realize that the New World was not a totally class-free country at all.

Castle Garden, a former fort built in 1811, was the first institution where the immigrants had to pass through before they entered the country. New York became the main immigration port during the 19th century. After Castle Garden became too small for the masses of people, Ellis Island functioned as the immigrant station, allowing or refusing people to enter the United States.

The arrival of the immigrants with their ships after a long journey is mentioned in Dos Passos' *Manhattan Transfer*: "The ferry passed close to a tubby steamer that rode at anchor listing towards Stan so that he could see all the decks. An Ellis Island tug was alongside. A stale smell came from the decks packed with upturned faces like a load of melons" (Dos Passos, 1953, p.251).

On January 1st, 1892 the Irish immigrant Annie Moore was the first person who passed the gates of Ellis Island. At its zenith this immigration station could check several thousands of passengers each day.

The "Great Hall" played the most important role on Ellis Island. It served as the main immigration registration with several counters, where people had to queue up in long lines until they were investigated by officers. The inspection hall next to it also had a significant function. Here the immigrants were checked by doctors for mental and physical diseases. These two sections were located in the main building.

Furthermore, the island provided a luggage depository, a ticket counter for trains, grocery stores, waiting rooms, custody rooms, offices, special examination rooms, a restaurant, a hospital, a sleeping hall, a bath and washing house and a power station. Later on there was also an employment agency located on the immigration station, where the immigrants could find a job immediately after their arrival.

The newcomers had to be very patient. After a long journey on an overcrowded ship they also had to wait for many hours until they were finally investigated by the officers on Ellis Island. The doctors there especially looked for tuberculosis and trachoma, a certain eye disease respectively a kind of conjunctivitis which can cause blindness. Immigrants who seemed to have diseases and needed further examination got a chalk sign on their clothes, an identification which had a discriminating and segregating effect.

Since 1917 investigations on Ellis Island became stricter and people had to wait even longer on the 'island of hope and tears'. Some regarded the immigration port as a prison with inhuman and undignified conditions, others, however, who had experienced even worse circumstances in their home country, depicted the place as the golden door to their new paradise named America where they finally had enough to eat.

In 1954 Ellis Island was closed for good. Since 1976 the former immigration station functions, together with the Statue of Liberty and Liberty Island, as one of the most important, impressive and moving immigration museums of the country.

> Bei unserer Ankunft in der Neuen Welt wurden wir als erstes auf Ellis Island interniert, wo die Einwanderungsbeamten uns wie eine Herde Vieh inspizierten (The director Josef von Sternberg about his arrival in America in 1924. In Besel and Kulgemeyer, 1986, p.16)

"Ellis Island is a place of names. Here millions of immigrants called out theirs for the first time [...] before they stepped ashore onto America's soil. To most, Ellis Island was an Isle of Hope, a brief stopping point on the way to a better life. To an unfortunate few, it became an Isle of Tears, a place of detention and possible rejection" (Hamblin, 1994, p.5).

Between 1897 and 1938 the island was the first step for many thousands of immigrants to enter the United States. It was the first time they came to America and here the decision was made, if they had to leave this country again.

> A ferry was leaving the immigrant station, a murmur rustled through the crowd that packed the edges of the wharf. "Deportees... It's the communists the Department of Justice is having deported... deportees... Reds. ...It's the Reds they are deporting." [...] "They are sending the Reds back to Russia." A handkerchief waved on the ferry, a red handkerchief. [...] ...Deportees. ...Agitators. ...Undesirables." [...] A sound of singing came from the ferryboat getting small, slipping away across the water. *C'est la lutte finale, groupons-nous et demain L'Internationale sera le genre humain.* "Take a look at the deportees. ... Take a look at the undesirable aliens," shouted the man with the telescopes and

field glasses. A girl's voice burst out suddenly, *"Arise prisoners of starvation,"* "Sh. ...They could pull you for that." The singing trailed away across the water. At the end of marbled wake the ferryboat was shrinking into haze. *International ... shall be the human race.* (Dos Passos, 1953, p.289/90)

The Statue of Liberty is deeply connected with immigration since its opening in 1886. The green lady with the torch left a nostalgic and glorifying impression in many immigrants' memories since this impressive and heroic statue was their symbol of the Promised Land, the symbol for freedom and all opportunities.

There is a plate on the base of the Statue of Liberty with a famous poem of the Jewish authoress Emma Lazarus on it. The lady who enlightened the New World for the immigrants is described as the "Mother of Exiles".

The immigrants associated America with the hope for a better life, with paradise where milk and honey were floating in the streets, with the land of freedom and endless possibilities, where everybody gets the chance to transform from rags to riches and where the streets were paved with gold and everything was beautiful. These hopes which people brought along with them on their arrival in America were often disappointed when they had to face reality. Anzia Yezierska, a Jewish immigrant, described her hopes and later her disappointment in the book *How I Found America*:

> Steerage – dirty bundles – foul odors – seasick humanity – but I saw and heard nothing of the foulness and ugliness around me. I floated in showers of sunshine; visions upon visions of the new world opened before me. From lips to lips flowed the golden legend of the golden country: "In America you can say what you feel – you can voice your thoughts in the open streets without fear of a Cossack." "In America is a home for everybody. The land is your land. Not like in Russia where you feel yourself a stranger in the village where you were born and raised – the village in which your father and grandfather lie buried." "Everybody is with everybody alike, in America. Christians and Jews are brothers together." "An end to the worry for bread. An end to the fear of the bosses over you. Everybody can do what he wants with his life in America." [...] "Plenty for all. Learning flows free like milk and honey." "Learning flows

free." The words painted pictures in my mind. I saw before me free schools, free colleges, free libraries, where I could learn and learn and keep on learning. In our village was a school, but only for Christian children. In the schools of America I'd lift up my head and laugh and dance – a child with other children. Like a bird in the air, from sky to sky, from star to star, I'd soar and soar. "Land! Land!" came the joyous shout. "America! We're in America!" cried my mother, almost smothering us in her rapture. All crowded and pushed on deck. They strained and stretched to get the first glimpse of the "golden country," lifting their children on their shoulders that they might see beyond them. Men fell on their knees to pray. Women hugged their babies and wept. Children danced. Strangers embraced and kissed like old friends. Old men and women had in their eyes a look of young people in love. Age-old visions sang themselves in me – songs of freedom of an oppressed people. America! – America!
(Yezierska, 1991, p.112/113)

The parallel existence of hope and disillusion is intensely described by Yezierska when she says: "I didn't come to America to turn into a machine. I came to America to make from myself a person. [...] What for did I come to America but to go to school – to learn – to think – to make something beautiful from my life..." (Yezierska, 1991, p.115).

The theme of not giving up, of working as hard as possible to finally make it, was always present among the immigrants and so the authoress writes: *"Dead generations whose faith though beaten back still presses on – a resistless, deathless force!* In this America that crushes and kills me, their spirit drives me on – to struggle – to suffer – but never to submit" (Yezierska, 1991, p.118).

In the short story 'Soap and Water' the guiding light of hope through all the pain and unexpected misery expresses itself from the bottom of her heart:

> Inside the ruin of my thwarted life, the *unlived* visionary immigrant hungered and thirsted for America. I had come a refugee from the Russian pogroms, aflame with dreams of America. I did not find America in the sweatshops, much less in the schools and colleges. But for hundreds of years the persecuted races all over the world were nurtured on hopes of America. [...] I saw all around me weary faces light

up with thrilling tales of the far-off "golden country." And so, though my faith in this so-called America was shattered, yet underneath, in the sap and roots of my soul, burned the deathless faith that America is, must be, somehow, somewhere. In the midst of my bitterest hatred and rebellions, visions of America rose over me, like songs of freedom of an oppressed people. My body was worn to the bone from overwork, my footsteps dragged with exhaustion, but my eyes still sought the sky, praying, ceaselessly praying, the dumb, inarticulate prayer of the lost immigrant: "America! Ach, America! Where is America?" (Yezierska.1991. p.173/74)

Most of the people who came to America intended to settle in this country and stay forever. There were, however, those who used the States as their second home where they could earn the money to live a good life back in their home country, maybe buy a piece of land or a house there. It is recorded that especially a lot of Italians practiced this way of living at the end of the 19th century.

Illustration of Annie Moore, the first immigrant to the United States to pass through the Ellis Island facility in New York Harbor, 1892.

The New Immigrant Depot. In: Irish World and American Industrial Liberator (New York, NY) Saturday, January 09, 1892; pg. 8; Issue 1,115; col A

Immigrants on a ship approaching New York City, bound for Ellis Island, with the Statue of Liberty in the background. Published in 1915 by Edwin Levick

Above: Danish emigrants at Larsen's Plads (Port of Copenhagen) leaving for America together with their relatives saying goodbye. Painted in 1890 by Edvard Petersen (1841–1911)

Below: Immigrants on deck of steamer "Germanic." Illus. in: Frank Leslie's illustrated newspaper, 1887 July 2, pp. 324-325. Library of Congress Prints and Photographs Division Washington, D.C. 20540 USA

500 workers from Poland are prohibited to enter the United States. Picture taken in 1930. Published in Bundesarchiv, Aktuelle-Bilder-Centrale, Georg Pahl (Bild 102)

Above: Immigrants just arrived from Foreign Countries--Immigrant Building, Ellis Island, New York Harbor. Picture taken in 1904 by Underwood & Underwood. Library of Congress Prints and Photographs Division.

Below: Immigrants seated on long benches, Main Hall, U.S. Immigration Station. Picture taken between 1907-1912. Photographs of Ellis Island. The New York Public Library.

Algerian immigrant to the United States.
Photographed on Ellis Island by Augustus F. Sherman. Between 1905 and 1920.
Published in: William Williams papers, Photographs of immigrants.
New York Public Library.

Ellis Island Immigration Station. Children from Lapland or Sweden.
Photograph by Augustus Francis Sherman (1865–1925).
Published in: William Williams papers, Photographs of immigrants,
created date: ca. 1906-1914.
New York Public Library.

A young Greek-American immigrant on Ellis Island, New York late 19th-20th century - Hulton Archive

A Turkish immigrant in New York (1912).
Photographer Augustus Francis Sherman (1865–1925).
New York Public Library, 1908.

Albanian Soldier.
Photographer Augustus Francis Sherman [ca. 1906-1914].
Published in William Williams papers, Photographs of immigrants
The New York Public Library.

Cossack man from the steppes of Russia.
Photographer Augustus Francis Sherman [ca. 1906-1914].
Published in William Williams papers, Photographs of immigrants
The New York Public Library.

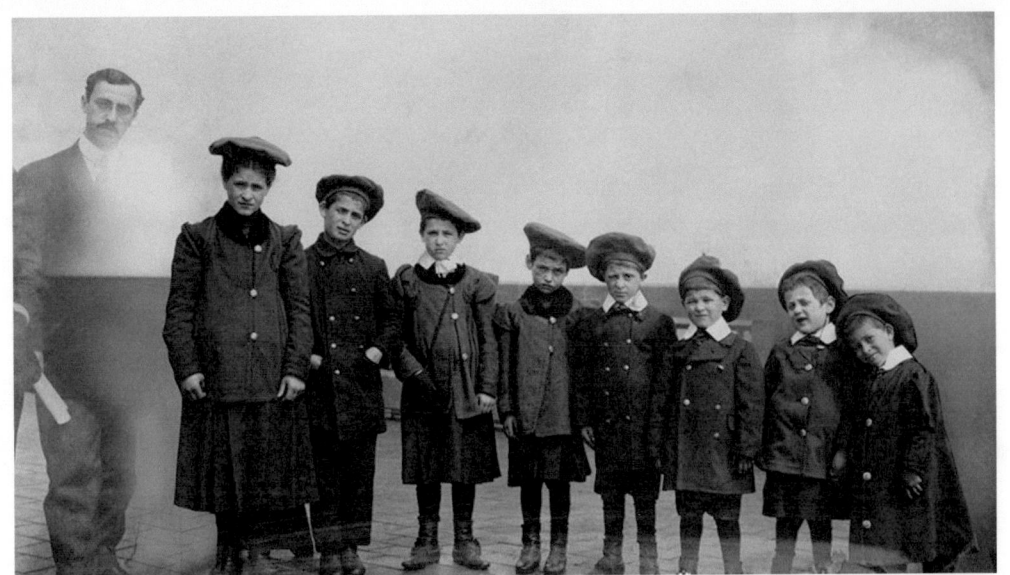

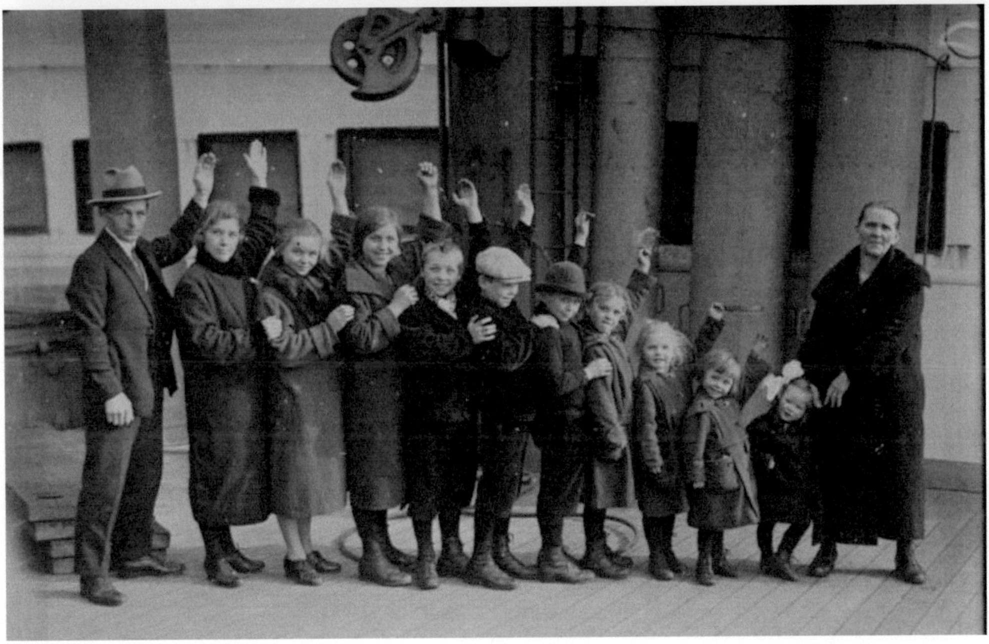

Above:
A man stands next to orphaned Russian Jews upon immigration to the U.S., New York, July 1919. Photographs of National Geographic.

Below:
From the smallest to the Largest!
An immigrant family with 10 children on their arrival at the port of New York. They want to try their luck in the new world.
1929
Bundesarchiv, Bild 102-08903 / CC-BY-SA

Above:
Immigrant children, Ellis Island, New York.
1908
Records of the Public Health Service. (90-G-125-29) / US GOV National Archives.
By Brown Brothers.

Left:
Italian immigrant mother with two children.
1913
Published in Popular Science Monthly,
Volume 83.

III. Five Points, Tenements and Sweatshops: The Living Conditions

> Through the smell of the arbutus she caught for a second the unwashed smell of his body, the smell of immigrants, of Ellis Island, of crowded tenements. [...] She could feel the huddling smell, spreading in dark slow crouching masses like corruption oozing from broken sewers, like a mob. (Dos Passos, 1953, p.395)

"By the 1830s the chasm between New York's rich and the elegant life of Fifth Avenue, and the city's poor, living in slums such as Five Points, was deepening" (Homberger, 1998, p.81).

When immigrants started to enter the city of New York in masses, the population suddenly exploded from less than one hundred thousand inhabitants to half a million souls. And they all needed a place to live. Within a very short amount of time homes had to be organized for the newcomers. The Lower East Side turned out to be the first mass habitation for the immigrants who managed to pass the strict inspections on Ellis Island.

Tenant-houses, which are now known as tenements, were established to solve the housing crisis. "Older single-family homes were "packed" with sub-tenants – immigrants looking for cheap accommodation – and within a brief period a Federal merchant's home could be turned into a slum property housing dozens of people" (Homberger, 1998, p.78).

The "rear house" was the first known tenement which was built for the purpose of crowding up dozens of people in it. These buildings were sometimes erected in the garden or backyard of another house which itself became a further tenement. The rear houses were often made of wood. At first they were only two stories high. However, the city built some further stories onto it, when extra space was needed to harbor more people. And "where two families had lived ten moved in" (Riis, 1971, p.6).

These additional buildings offered the possibility to increase "the density of population without greatly altering the city's appearance" (Homberger, 1998, p.110). The brick buildings in front of the backyard rear houses once used to inhabitate the aristocracy of Manhattan. When they moved away and the buildings were managed by real-estate agents and boarding-house keepers, the former "*large* rooms were partitioned into *several smaller ones,* without regard to light or ventilation, the rate of rent being lower in proportion to space or height from the street; and they soon became filled from cellar to garret with a class of tenantry living from hand to mouth, loose in morals, improvident in habits, degraded, and squalid as beggary itself" (Riis, 1971, p.5).

Often one family of seven or more members had to share one single small room which served as kitchen, living- and bed-room. In many cases this room was also used as the place of work, often a private kind of sweatshop where the women worked during the day. There was hardly enough light or fresh air in most of the rooms since the small chambers, which were a result of the division of large rooms, often had no windows.

A bathroom usually was provisional and mostly outside in a small backyard. It was a stopgap solution which made it almost impossible to live a hygienic life. Inside the tenement buildings there often was no running water in the apartments. Normally, sinks could be found outside in the hallway where they had to be used by the whole floor. And most of the time they were broken or just unbelievably dirty.

Others had no sink at all and were forced to use water pumps on the ground floor to get some water.

The tenants lived without any comfort. Safety was also not part of the contract. The owners of the tenements just cared about the rent and were not interested at all in improving the living conditions for those who had to live in these barracks.

Since people were crowded like animals in the narrow and unventilated dark rooms of the buildings, diseases spread rapidly. In blocks such as Gotham Court a cholera epidemic which hardly affected the clean parts of New York killed hundreds of tenants. The living conditions were the optimum birthplace for all kinds of bacteria and getting sick meant ordinary life for the immigrants in the tenements.

In these areas of the city the mortal rate was higher than in the whole state of New York and the sad statistic gives evidence that the majority of New York City's population lived under such inhuman circumstances.

When improvements were made, people had toilets, windows and running water in their apartments, but still no bath in most cases. However, not only the slums in Lower Manhattan offered the city's worst living conditions. There were also rotten tenement apartments in Harlem and Brooklyn like in Red Hook, Williamsburg and Brownsville which were in some cases described as even worse than the Lower East Side tenements. Today, immigration brings along different faces, however, not much different conditions.

Anzia Yezierska writes about the disappointment she felt when she arrived at her new home, a tenement building on the Lower East Side:

> I looked about the narrow streets of squeezed-in stores and houses, ragged clothes, dirty bedding oozing out of the windows, ash-cans and garbage-cans cluttering the side-walks. A vague sadness pressed down my heart – the first doubt of America. "Where are the green fields and open spaces in America?" cried my heart. "Where is the golden country of my dreams?" A loneliness for the fragrant silence of the woods that lay beyond our mud hut welled up in my heart, a longing for the soft, responsive earth of our village streets. All about me was the hardness of brick and stone, the stinking smells of crowded

poverty. [...] In America were rooms without sunlight, rooms to sleep in, to eat in, to cook in, but without sunshine. [...] And where was there a place in America for me to play? I looked out into the alley below and saw pale-faced children scrambling in the gutter. "Where is America?" cried my heart. (Yezierska, 1991, p.113/114)

Yezierska, the writer of the book *How I found America* which includes the story "Hungry Hearts" where the quotation above is taken from, describes her personal immigrant experiences in this story. She talks about the enormous disillusion she was confronted with when she had to face the fact that the America of her dreams had nothing in common with the real country. This disappointment is possibly responsible for her distorted and restless self, which is not able to feel satisfaction and having a home throughout her life.

By 1855 half a million people populated the tenements of New York City. The Lower East Side which had 290,000 inhabitants in one single square mile remained "the most densely populated district in all the world, China not excluded,"[2] for a long period of time.

The living conditions which caused all kinds of diseases and often also death were below every human being's dignity. However, the rents of the tenements were up to 30 percent higher than for a nice uptown apartment. The inhabitants' life was as well degrading and expensive. The Society for the Improvement of the Condition of the Poor described the situation with these words: "Crazy old buildings, crowded rear tenements in filthy yards, dark, damp basements, leaking garrets, shops, outhouses, and stables converted into dwellings, though scarcely fit to shelter brutes, are habitations of thousands of our fellow-beings in this wealthy, Christian city" (in Riis, 1971, p.11).

Examples of small rooms were five families, "twenty persons of both sexes and all ages"[3] shared two beds and had to live without any chair, table, screen or partition, were not the exception. Often people lived in cellars like rats. Around the 1850s one could sometimes find up to 80 children in one single tenement and several years later there were even up to 180 people living or just sleeping in two tenement buildings.

---

[2] Riis, Jacob A. *How the Other Half Lives*. 1971. p.6
[3] Riis, Jacob A. *How the Other Half Lives.* 1971. p.6-8

Improvement of the verminous accommodations full of lice and bacteria did not start before the 1860s when already 15,000 tenements existed throughout the city.

After the Civil War people became aware of the horrible conditions in the tenements and they started to do something against it. However, it was a long way until the circumstances of the inhabitants could really be improved. The Metropolitan Board of Health was founded due to a citizens' movement in 1867 and the "Tenement-House Act" evolved which was the first step of improvement. The Board was given certain and important rights to investigate the housing conditions and to seize sanitary measures. It was a long and stony way until one could talk of a real amendment of the tenement living conditions and this was only the beginning.

Since 1879 it was against the law to have completely dark rooms, and so windows and airshafts had to be added to the single chambers. In spite of the apartments themselves, the Board of Health proposed to widen up the most rotten and decayed streets. This way, disreputable and infamous quarters like the Five Points or Mulberry Bend were eliminated after a while. However, the tenement improvement was one of the hardest problems the reformers and the city were confronted with.

The fast growth of population, the uncountable number of unemployed or badly paid people, and the difficulty to call the owners of the tenements to account for the terrible conditions of their buildings, all resulted in the fact that there were still 42,700 tenement houses on Manhattan Island by 1900 with 1,585,000 inhabitants living in them.

The owners of the tenements who were angry about any expenses they had to make, as well as the tenants themselves who had adapted to their surroundings after a generation of protest and were finally content to stay in these places, built the opposition to the reforms since they both believed that "official interference [means] an infringement of personal rights, and a hardship" (Riis, 1971, p.13). However, the Board of Health finally succeeded, even though they had to use the police sometimes to get the tenants out of their cellars, chambers and caves. Still, problems were not easy to handle and the situation seemed to get worse every single day.

Life inside the tenements and its surroundings was often contradicting. Many immigrants worked hard to find a way out of the ghetto. Most of them never gave up the hope of a better life. However, there were also those who resigned and therefore supported the criminal and dissolute character of the districts.

The alleys and courts of huge and overcrowded brick buildings or wooden rear houses in the backyards which were connected with each other through hundreds of clothes-lines (as if the inhabitants were continually fighting against the dirt and foulness they could not get rid of), seemed to be the birthplace of criminals and every day a new bunch of them ascended out of the gutter.

And after ten years of improving the living conditions in the buildings, the people were at least in the same social situation like before. The darkness of the surroundings, the gutter-like atmosphere in the dirty and unhealthy accommodations had affected the moral of the inhabitants and this could not be changed by cutting windows into the brick.

Corruption, crime, violence, brutality, prostitution and other immoralities were dominating the tenement quarters like Five Points. And when a radical cleaning changed Five

Points' evil character in some basic sense, there were still other areas like the Mulberry Street Bend which functioned as the centre of crime and an immoral living.

These criminal forces resulted from the fact that people had not cared about the tenements and their inhabitants for a very long time. They had forgotten these poor members of their young society and now they had to face the outcome which was not about to stop anymore. Riis says that "it is one of the curses of the tenement-house system that the worst houses exercise a levelling influence upon all the rest, just as one bad boy in a school-room will spoil the whole class" (Riis, 1971, p.14). And so, despite all the improvements like windows, air-shafts or cleaning a whole quarter, the official organizations could not eliminate criminality, poverty and "outrageous overcrowding" which described the characteristics of the tenements.

The 19th century brought along about a dozen known and certainly much more unknown street gangs in Manhattan, all involved in the criminal activities of the city. The age of gangsters, gambling, political corruption, murder, drug-dealing, and vice had begun on a large scale in the streets of New York during the 1820s. And over 100 years later it was still present, especially in the Italian Mafia, with Charles 'Lucky' Luciano and Meyer Lansky as the most important, powerful and famous representatives in New York, collaborating with the families of Chicago where Al Capone was ruling the scene in the early 20th century.

Often judges, politicians, and the police were open to bribery and therefore supported the criminal wheeling and dealing as well as dark machinations of gangs, gamblers, dealers and so on. The local gangs fought each other and murders became ordinary life. The gangland of New York found its members in the tenements of the city, in the corruptible, lawless and dirty quarters like Five Points and other slums of the Lower East Side. The bosses were often part of the old Sicilian Mafia in New York, or of other groups of the organized crime.

> "Suffolk Street is in the very thick of the battle for breath. For it lies in the heart of that part of the East Side which has within the last two or three decades become the Ghetto of the American metropolis, and, indeed, the metropolis of the Ghettos of the world. It is one of the most densely populated spots on the face of the earth – a seething human sea fed by streams, streamlets, and rills of

immigration flowing from all the Yiddish-speaking centers of Europe. [...] – all come in search of fortune." (Cahan, 1970, p.13/14)

The tenements have always been split up into little districts which consisted of single courts and alleys with their own names. These tenement districts all had an individual character which separated them from the others. The division of the tenements made the evolution of diverse ethnic quarters which soon followed the habitation of the tenements during the first big immigration wave, easy and unavoidable.

Some of the most famous districts were called the Five Points, Gotham Court (part of Cherry Street in the 7th ward with the worst reputation), Blind Man's Alley, the "Barracks" in Mott Street, Cherry Street itself, Fourth Ward and the Mulberry Street Bend, also known as "The Bend" which was demolished in the 1890s and which belonged to the "Bloody Sixth" ward on the Lower East Side.

All these districts had their own sad and horrible little records like Gotham Court which inhabited almost 1,000 people at the same time. Here, the mortal rate was higher than anywhere else in the state and epidemics killed people during times when the rest of the city was free of these diseases.

In Gotham Court a sanitary official once found 146 sick people infected with all kinds of illnesses during one single counting in 1862. And within three years of observation he reported that 61 children out of 138 had died during that time, most of them before they were one year old. Children died of measles and other diseases, mostly because of the darkness of the bedrooms which took the last chance from the child to survive.

It was not only the unhygienic and filthy surrounding and the fact that no doctor or medicine was available who or which could cure the ill child; the problem was that the mortal rate in windowless rooms is one hundred percent higher than in places where the sunlight gets a chance to shine through.

In Blind Man's Alley blind and poor tenants lived under the most horrible conditions in dirty and rotten apartments sparing any kind of comfort and hygiene. The landlord who had made an unbelievable fortune of 400,000 dollars grew blind himself and fought against the new regulations of the Board of Health as long as possible.

In Cherry Street murder was "nothing to 'make a fuss' about"[4] and corruption, crime or immorality belonged to the tenement district's everyday life. The Fourth Ward held the record of having "turned out more criminals than all the rest of the city together" (Riis, 1971, p.34).

Slums like Five Points had already existed before the arrival of the huge immigration waves. Most of the 12,000 Afro-Americans of New York had lived here. In the late 1820s there was no slavery anymore, but racial segregation and discrimination still existed very lively. Very soon, with the start of the immigration waves, Five Points became the best-known district of the city. It was notorious because of the dilapidation and overcrowding of its accommodations, its unbridled street life and its multicultural population streaming into the city from all over the world. After a while one could find any kind of skin color, nationality, gender and age in this area.

---

[4] Riis, Jacob A. *How the Other Half Lives*. 1971. p.34

Five Points was originally planned for middle class people, but since it was built too hastily on an old sanitary landfill, the single buildings began to sink after a while and the inhabitants left the place. Afterwards the quarter was populated by the poor who could not afford another place to live.

The cholera broke out in New York in 1832 and mostly affected the new slums of the island where the disease found most of its victims. 3513 people were killed in the course of the epidemic; most of them were poor immigrants. Besides, these newcomers were also held responsible for the tragedy. However, it is not a secret that the inhuman living conditions caused this disease and others to follow.

Fernando Wood who used to be the mayor of New York City in the 1840s and 1850s was often associated with the slum life of the city, the horrible living conditions, and the criminal situation in the tenement districts of New York.

Two parts of the metropolis described Wood's New York the best: the Tombs and Five Points. The first one was the prison of the city which was situated on Centre Street, between the Bowery and Broadway. The second one was just a few blocks away and was said to be the worst slum in the world. The whole area was known as being rough and dangerous and a city guide book from that time wrote: "From Canal to Chatham Street there is not the slightest sign of cleanliness or comfort" (in Homberger, 1998, p.84).

The Tombs had the function to regulate Five Points, since this tenement quarter was one of the dirtiest, most criminal and most violent parts of the city, inhabiting mostly immigrants. The prison which was built in the 1830s was the answer of the city towards poverty and lawlessness in the rotten tenement areas which represented the city to a great extent during Fernando Wood's times.

Slum life was the key term while Wood was the head of the metropolis. Life of the poor was dominated and therefore degraded by prostitution and liquor stores. Besides having to live in overcrowded tenements, people were confronted with saloons, rum shops and dozens of brothels which supported the criminality in those quarters and which almost needed to come up due to the people's nearly hopeless life with hardly any positive prospects.

This way the vicious circle found its beginning since alcohol and prostitution were often the only joy the poor had in their miserable life. And there was no other district comparable to Five Points which fulfilled all these negative stereotypes for itself. Eric Homberger describes this tenement area the following way:

> Five Points, around the intersection of Park Street and Worth, was a warren of narrow streets and decayed, foul-smelling buildings with a nationwide reputation for murder and vice. At its heart was the Old Brewery, a tenement in which rooms cost $2 to $10 per month and which housed uncounted hundreds in the greatest squalor. It was the most densely occupied building in the city, containing at one time 1,200 persons. In the eyes of the city, those who lived there were poor, verminous, uneducated, and degraded by poverty, intemperance and vice. They were largely of foreign origin. (Homberger, 1998, p.84)

However, the ghettos of the Lower East Side were not only crowded with a corruptive, criminal and immoral breed.

Many of the immigrants worked and learned all day and night long to flee the slums of the city as soon as possible.

Besides, the districts did not only function as the meeting point of New York's gangsters, but also as a place where traditions and old values, as well as communities of the different ethnic groups came together and felt at home.

"Work, work, and more work – the classic immigrant story seems to be repeating itself as a new group of arrivals enters New York" (Foner, 2000, p.105). The immigrants worked hard to gain a foothold in the new nation. However, in most cases working conditions for the immigrants could be described as terrible, especially in factories or businesses owned by other nationalities.

Besides the tenements there were other places which supported a miserable and harsh life. Sweatshops were spread all over the city, employing cheap laborers to achieve a higher profit. A lot of immigrants, especially Jewish immigrant women and children used to work in the garment industry. They worked in the factories themselves or at home in their own small apartments. Adults and children usually worked from sunrise till sunset at their sewing machines.

Sweatshops were small garment factories or workshops which could be found in small tenement apartments or loft buildings. They were crowded, without any heater for the cold winters or ventilation for hot summer days, and the light inside the factory hall was so dim that most workers destroyed their eyes during the years of their employment. The immigrant workers were poorly paid and they had to work from early in the morning until late in the evening.

The women who worked in the sweatshops founded the ILGWU (International Ladies Garment Workers Union) in 1900, but they did not manage to really improve the situation in the shops until a fire on March 25, 1911 killed 146 immigrants who worked at the Triangle Shirtwaist Company. Many of the workers died because there was no fire escape and no door open which they could have used to rescue themselves. Nobody could enter or leave the building. After this tragedy a lot of reforms were made to improve the buildings and working conditions as well as fire-code safety regulations.

Apart from the sweatshops immigrants were deeply integrated in manufacturing and the construction boom. The Grand Central Terminal, for example, was mainly built by Italians. Working on the docks by loading and unloading coal or goods from and onto the ships was also mostly done by immigrants. The Irish had the monopoly on this and other businesses.

With regard to the pushcart boom among the immigrants Foner says: "All day and into the evening, Orchard Street, Hester Street, Grand Street, and Rivington Street were packed on both sides with continuous lines of pushcarts that extended from block to block" (Foner, 2000, p.83). Furthermore, the ethnic districts were crowded with several colorful stores selling all kinds of goods.

The Jewish immigrants belonged to the group which had the most urgent wish to become an active part of American life. Assimilation was highly important for many Jews and therefore a lot of them "attended night schools for citizenship classes and English" (Homberger, 1998, p.133). These schools spread all over Manhattan and between 1890 and 1910 there were already more than 24 of them only on the Lower East Side.

Different settlements like the University Settlement (1886), the College Settlement (1889) or the Nurses' Settlement (1893) came up. They had the aim to improve the situation for the immigrants on the Lower East Side by establishing public health services or housing reforms, and providing people with better education and recreational facilities. Children got kindergartens, playgrounds and even summer camps and a Visiting Nurse Service was also established.

Jacob A. Riis, the author of *How the Other Half Lives* was not only a photographer and journalist who documented the situation he had to experience himself when he came to the States as a Danish immigrant; he also functioned as a reformer who organized campaigns for the improvement of the living conditions on the Lower East Side. The result was that some of the worst slums were demolished in the 1890s to build parks and playgrounds. Mulberry Bend which used to be one of the most disastrous tenement districts of all was one of the first to be abolished.

Settlement houses were schools which were established to teach the new arrivals from abroad in the American way of life and provide them with special abilities and expertise they needed to have success in the New World. These schools were led by liberal reformers which had the aim to involve the diverse and poor ethnic immigrants into the customs, traditions and values of America and its prevailing class. Clarence Karier wrote that they needed to be "Americanized so as to protect the 'American way'" (in Yezierska, Salome of the Tenements, p. XIV).

The survival of the existing society was in danger according to the reform activists and they tried to transform the newcomers into American subjects under the guise of charity and selfless educators. This fear of an endangered American society was based on the immigrants' persistence in living their own culture, their own values and customs in America. Assimilation and Americanization was the goal.

This manipulation of the immigrants also brought about the progress of the country. The newcomers who learned to fit in supplied their new home country with cheap labor force and this led to economic growth.

Since the huge influx of new inhabitants provided the United States with many unskilled workers, the need for machines increased which helped to make work easier and feasible by almost everybody. This was the beginning of the industrialization and mass production. America started to become a rich nation with the help of cheap work forces.

Parallels between contemporary immigrants and the masses from the 19th and early 20th century can be drawn by taking a look at the living conditions, jobs or discrimination. Unfortunately not much has changed in some areas of the city, even though the districts had moved to other parts of the island or its neighboring boroughs. One can still find overcrowded, decayed and run down apartments which are contaminated with vermin and faeces. Tenements such as those decayed hovels of the 19th and early 20th century have been abolished and demolished, but the poor of the city, who are often immigrants, sometimes still have to live with cockroaches and emphysema as their daily companions.

Public Housing was a step taken by the city to create a better living situation for the people. Today, the metropolis has already built thousands of such apartments and is still planning new housing projects. However, the majority of today's immigrants can tell a nice lower-middle-class house their own.

In John Dos Passos' novel *Manhattan Transfer* poverty and immigration are also involved into the plot, even though this is not the book's topic. The novel deals with the city itself and makes use of a wide range of characters and themes. It can be described as a chronicle of 30 years of New York from 1890 until 1920. The characters are more or less figures on the surface of the main protagonist which is the city itself. They are like "puppets" and "mechanical toys" of the city which uses them for its purposes and spits them out afterwards.

In this complex New York (hi)story the topic of immigration sometimes occurs as a part of the city, something that exists in it. One hears Congo talking about freedom, equality, progress, prosperity, promise and the land of hope for the immigrants when he says: "I want to get somewhere in the world, that's what I mean. Europe's rotten and stinking. In America a fellow can get ahead. Birth dont matter, education dont matter. It's all getting ahead" (Dos Passos, 1953, p.21).

The machine-like city spits out those who are not able to fit in. Those who couldn't make it in the metropolis and who got lost in the whirl of the fast moving glittering city feel the urge of leaving: " '...I'd be a appy man sir, if I could get back to the old country. This arent any plyce for an old man, it's for the young and strong, this is.' He drew a gout-twisted hand across the bay and pointed to the statue. 'Look at er, she's alookin towards Hengland she is.'" (Dos Passos, 1953, p.63).

Above:
Two boys asleep at 2 a.m. in the press room of the "Sun" newspaper.
1892 by Jacob Riis (1849-1914).

Below:
Children sleeping in Mulberry Street.
1890 by Jacob Riis (1849-1914).

Above:
"Bandit's Roost, 1890, New York City." Photograph by Jacob Riis, featured in his book How the Other Half Lives (1890)

Below:
"The Tramp", Photograph by Jacob Riis, featured in his book How the Other Half Lives (1890)

Above:
Tenement of 1863, for Twelve Families on Each Flat. D, dark. L, light. H, halls.
Published in the book How the Other Half Lives (1890) by Jacob A. Riis.

Below:
New York, yard of tenement between 1900 and 1910.
US-Library Of Congress. Detroit Publishing Co.

"Baxter Street Alley, Rag-Picker's Row" In the February 12, 1898 issue of the New York Sun.

Jacob Riis wrote, "At 59 Baxter Street . . . is an alley leading in from the sidewalk with tenements on either side crowding so close as to almost shut out the light of day. On one side they are brick and on the other wood, but there is little difference in their ricketiness and squalor." -Jacob Riis, 1898

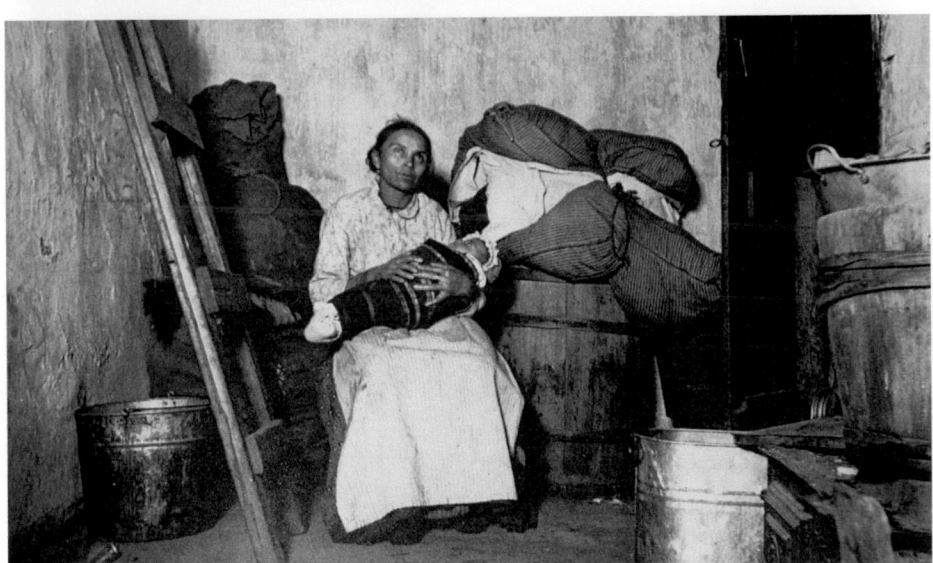

Above:
Jacob Riis, "Lodgers in a Crowded Bayard Street Tenement--'Five Cents a Spot'".
Ca. 1890-1900. Jacob August Riis (1849-1914)

Below:
"In the Home of an Italian Rag-Picker, Jersey Street", photograph by Jacob Riis (1849-
1914), taken around 1890.

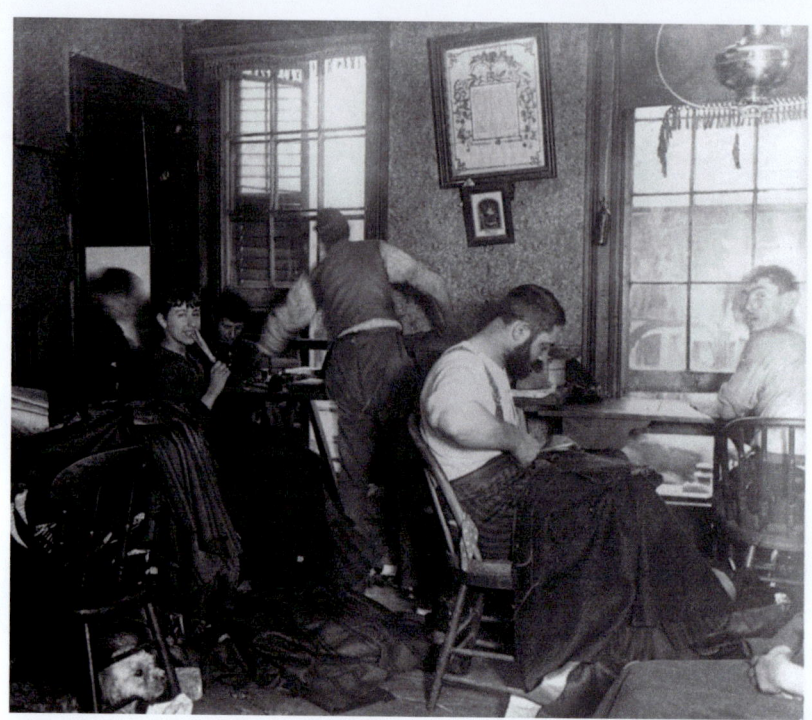

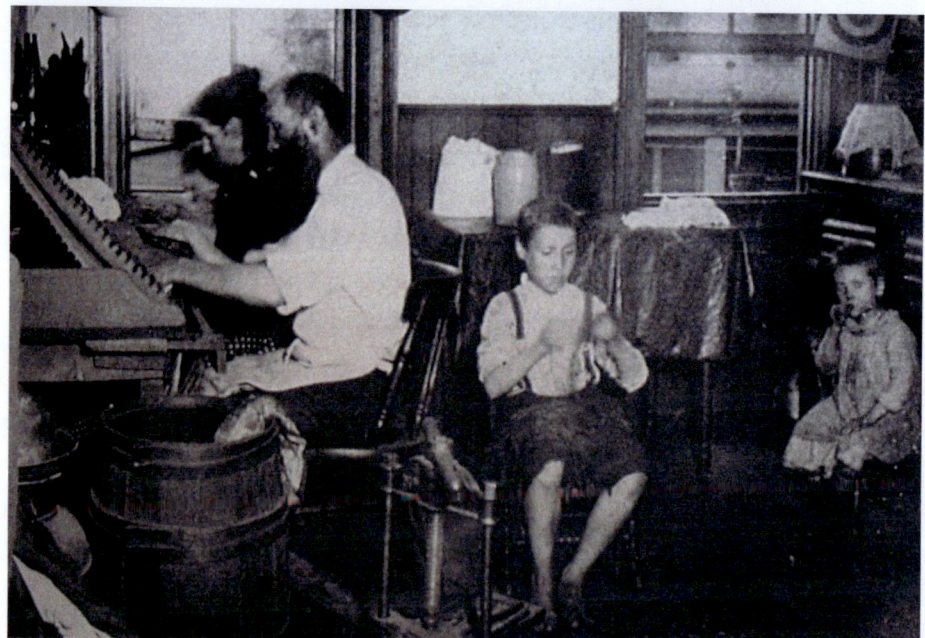

Above:
Workers in a sweatshop in Ludlow Street Tenement, New York City. Picture taken around 1889 by Jacob Riis. US-Library Of Congress

Below:
Bohemian cigarmakers at work in their tenement. Picture taken in 1890 by Jacob Riis. Brinkley, Douglas: History of the United States. Viking Penguin. New York, 1998. Page 227

81

Above:
Hells Kitchen and Sebastopol. Picture taken by Jacob Riis before 1890.

Below:
Peddlers and markets in Mulberry Street, New York City. Created and published around 1900. Detroit Publishing Co., no. 53641. Library of Congress.

Bottle Alley. Picture taken by Jacob Riis before 1890.

IV. From Little Italy to Chinatown: The Ethnic Districts Evolve

> In New York alone there are more persons of German descent than persons of native descent, and the German element is larger than in any city of Germany except Berlin. There are nearly twice as many Irish as in Dublin, about as many Jews as in Warsaw, and more Italians than in Naples or Venice (Robert Hunter, 1912 in Homberger, 1998, p.136).

New York is the biggest and most famous ethnic city in the world. After masses of Germans and Irish arrived in the mid 19th century, the "new immigration" of the late 19th and early 20th century (1880-1920) mostly brought huge masses of Russian Jews and Italians to the New World. For many of these immigrants the Statue of Liberty was the first sight of their future home country they got a glimpse of.

By 1920 the city had about ten major ethnic groups which had found together in several ethnic districts. The Chinese settled below the Bowery, the Syrian, Turkish and American Greek had found their new home on the tip of the island along the Hudson River, the Russian, Polish and other Jews could be found on the whole East Side of Lower Manhattan (from the Bowery to the East River, over Houston Street up to Union Square and Third Avenue at 25th Street), and they had also a large district close to the Bronx and Harlem in the east and north of Central Park North. Little quarters could also be found close to the East River as well as near the Hudson River in Midtown Manhattan.

The Italians were by that time spread all over the city. Big parts of their districts surrounded Chinatown, took large parts of Greenwich and the East Village, could be found along the Hudson and East River and had also large areas Uptown, east of Central Park.

Large districts of the Irish were along the two rivers, mostly Downtown and Midtown Manhattan. The French had found their new home in Midtown, close to Broadway and on the Upper West Side. German districts could mostly be found along the East River, in Yorkville and up to Harlem and the Bronx. The Czech and Hungarian had established on the East River of Midtown Manhattan, the Scandinavian and Finnish had their home close to Madison Square and the African-American could mostly be found in little quarters along the West Side of Manhattan up to the Bronx.

Most of the immigrants of the 19th and early 20th century came from Europe. Even later on in the 1960s this trend was still topical. In 1900 more than 90 percent of all immigrants were Europeans. This was also because of several laws which tried to keep racial and religious mix down. After the immigration restriction laws in the first decades of the 20th century the city became less "foreign".

Only in 1965 with the enforcement of the Hart-Celler Act immigration started with new and more power again. The possibility of reuniting families brought many new immigrants along and a new wave of immigration started with the Chinese becoming more powerful and South- and Middle Americans beginning to stream into the city. The Asian and Hispanic population of the city rose to a great extent.

"In 1990, for the first time in the city's history, no single race or ethnic group formed a majority of the city's inhabitants" (Homberger, 1998, p.160). Soon the city was filled with Arabs, Chinese, Koreans, Haitians, Jamaicans, Guyanese, Dominicans, Mexicans, as well as immigrants from all parts of Africa, South America and Europe. In a school in

Elmhurst, Queens, more than 30 languages were spoken by students in the 1980-1990s.

"Since 1900, more than 33 million aliens have been admitted to the United States as immigrants. The immigrant population of New York has remained three or four times above the national level" (Homberger, 1998, p.163).

The old tenement areas which were inhabited by a mixed crowd of immigrants (usually not one single individual there was "native-born"), were mostly downtown, close to the central business area. The immigrants 'chose' this place because they needed to be close to their places of work which were often uncertain and where they had to work very long each day. Transportation was not as developed as it is today; the subway was not ready yet.

Districts like "Jewtown" on the Lower East Side were dirty, unsafe and unhealthy with unreasonable living conditions. However, here the immigrants lived with their friends, relatives and people from the same ethnic or national background, people who had the same customs and traditions, spoke the same language, and helped new arrivals with finding a job or accommodation.

These districts of New York were mostly responsible for the cosmopolitan character of the city. In the alleys and courts of these quarters one could find a diversity of different cultures, nationalities and ethnic groups. And within a very short amount of time little colonies developed where these various groups came and lived together.

As early as 1890 there were already dozens of diverse nations among the immigrants and they turned the city into a colorful painting, having a wider spectrum than the colors of a rainbow.

The first Chinese settlement had already existed in 1830 in the harbor of New York. Jacob A. Riis mentions Italians, Germans, Frenchmen, Africans, Spaniards, Russians, Scandinavians, Jews, Arabs, Greeks, Chinamen and even some Native Americans (people from Indian tribes like the Iroquois), which all found together in small groups and soon spread throughout the whole island, turning streets and areas into their specific quarters. The evolution of the ethnic districts had found its beginning.

Riis states that there was no "distinctively American community" in New York, especially in the tenement areas.

He writes that the original Americans, which one can define as the early settlers or, even though not everybody is in agreement with that, as the early immigrants who helped founding the nation, seemed to have disappeared or have become invisible due to the masses streaming into the city by then.

This first big immigration wave which occurred in the course of Riis' life brought new cultures and ethnicities to New York that started to conquer the city and began to form the character of the metropolis totally new. Riis puts this development the following way: "In their [the native-born American's] place has come this queer conglomerate mass of heterogeneous elements, ever striving and working like whiskey and water in one glass, and with the like result: final union and a prevailing taint of whiskey" (Riis, 1971, p.19).

These extremely poor newcomers were not all corrupt and criminal and a lot of them never gave up the hope with which they had come to this country. This hope had kept them alive and had finally brought success to some of them. Many of the immigrants could finally realize their personal American Dream by developing businesses, monopolizing them and living the free and independent life they had dreamt of, away from crowded tenements and sweatshops where they had to work hard and under inhuman conditions to earn a few pennies.

The development of the ethnic districts brought different advantages for the immigrants. They felt a unity among their people and they could stick to their traditions and practice them. Here, they did not have to be afraid to lose their roots completely, due to the cultural influences of their new home. The members of their community, their ethnic and cultural background and their heritage functioned as a memory for the immigrants which prevented them from forgetting the old values. Besides, the community of their own people helped them to avoid or stop feelings of loneliness or being totally lost between two worlds - the new and unknown one they had entered and the old one they had left behind.

However, there was also another side to the coin which meant isolation from and ignorance toward the new culture and nation, as well as an inability to assimilate to the unfamiliar surroundings by learning the language, dealing with people from other cultures or trying to get involved into the new society they had moved into.

It did not take very long until the Italians were known for their bakeries, corner fruit-stands, boot-blacking industry and later on for their Italian restaurants. The Chinese were identified with the laundry business and their food. The Irish were famous for bricklaying, saloons, pubs and their political activity. Later on one could state that a remarkably high number of police officers in New York were and still are of Irish descent. The Jews were known for being successful businessmen and tradesmen who have always belonged to those ruling the commercial district.

The shaping of the diverse districts was taking place in the rotten tenement areas of the city since the immigrants were still poor. The first step was the habitation of the tenements with more and more new arrivals from one single culture. And sooner or later certain districts were only crowded with people of one and the same cultural background.

This was the beginning of the creation of the miniature countries within the megalopolis, a start which took place in the slums of the city. Jacob A. Riis mentions the development of ethnic quarters in the late 19th century in his book *How the Other Half Lives*, however, influenced by negative stereotypes:

A map of the city, colored to designate nationalities, would show more stripes than on the skin of a zebra, and more colors than any rainbow. The city on such a map would fall into two great halves, green for the Irish prevailing in the West Side tenement districts, and blue for the Germans on the East Side. But intermingled with these ground colors would be an odd variety of tints that would give the whole the appearance of an extraordinary crazy-quilt. From down in the Sixth Ward, upon the site of the old Collect Pond [...], the red of the Italian would be seen forcing its way northward along the line of Mulberry Street to the quarter of the French purple on Bleecker Street and South Fifth Avenue, to lose itself and reappear, after a lapse of miles, in the "Little Italy" of Harlem, east of Second Avenue. [...] On the West Side the red would be seen overrunning the old Africa of Thompson Street, pushing the black of the negro rapidly uptown [...]. Hardly less aggressive than the Italian, the Russian and Polish Jew, having overrun the district between Rivington and Division Streets, east of the Bowery, [...] is filling the tenements of the old Seventh Ward to the river front, and disputing with the Italian every foot of available space in the back alley of Mulberry Street. [...] Between the dull gray of the Jew [...] and the Italian red, would be seen squeezed in on the map a sharp streak of yellow, marking the narrow boundaries of Chinatown. Dovetailed in with the German population, the poor but thrifty Bohemian might be picked out [...]. Down near the Battery the West Side emerald would be soiled by a dirty stain, spreading rapidly like a splash of ink on a sheet of blotting paper, headquarters of the Arab tribe [...]. Dots and dashes of color here and there would show where the Finnish sailors [...], the Greek [...], and the Swiss [...] [live]. And so on to the end of the long register, all toiling together in the galling fetters of the tenement. (Riis, 1971, p.20-22)

From all over the world immigrants streamed to New York to make it. The city was crowded with ambitious people who wanted to be a part of the "city's many industries or its commerce" (Homberger, 1998, p.94).

These newcomers were now rootless. They had left everything behind and started a totally new life in a strange world with different rules and conditions. This theoretically offered them the opportunity to adapt more easily to the upcoming future trend of their new home. Those who had been living in this society for generations certainly had difficulties in dealing with an overall change. However, this possibility does not imply that the reality was often much different, since rootlessness is also one of the biggest problems the immigrants had and still have to face today.

In the first generation immigrants often were and are not able to accept the new way of living and they stick to their traditions. This way they try to avoid getting lost in the oversized whirlpool of nationalities which had found a new home in this big and tremendous city. However, sometimes they lost or still lose themselves on the way, ending up as a culturally and socially homeless person with neither the old nor the new country assimilated to their lives.

Most of the early immigrants tried to keep up with their traditions, customs, values, and their sense of community. "They [...] applauded furiously at performances of plays which reflected their lives, read newspapers in their mother-tongues, and most decidedly told and retold family stories" (Homberger, 1998, p.94). And of course they wanted to stay within their own community, their own ethnic group and background to get a feeling of being at home and not being alone. Therefore the different ethnic quarters of New York City developed and many of them are still in lively and vivid existence.

The Irish tenements had evolved on the West Side, after their immigration had begun on a large scale in the 1840s, the German immigrants had found their new home in "Kleindeutschland" (Little Germany) which was situated on the East Side between the 10th and 17th ward, and the overcrowded slums of the Jewish and Italian immigrants could be found east of the Bowery.

> Was mir die alte Heimath neidisch versagt, hier hab ich's gefunden: Verdienst, Zufriedenheit, Familienglück und die beste Aussicht, daß es noch besser werde in der Zukunft. Gesegnet sei Dein Kommen in unser schönes, großes freies Land Amerika! Unten auf der Straße spielen die deutschen Musikanten, die jeden Abend durch unsere Straße ziehen, die begeisternde Weise des ,Star Spangled Banner'... (in Lang, 1988, p.130)

"Kleindeutschland" developed in the 1840s when about 40,000 Germans settled east of the Bowery along the East River in an area consisting of 400 blocks. Little Germany was the first compact district where only Germans lived in one single quarter. The Irish were the larger immigration group at that time, but their districts were mostly spread all over the city during the first couple of years.

For the Germans "Kleindeutschland", where their people were predominantly at home, meant an "extraordinary vitality". The commercial life of "Kleindeutschland" took place on Avenue B which was also known as "German Broadway". Here one could find small shops, basement factories and goods which were piled up on the sidewalks. Avenue A was responsible for the social life. Lager beer halls, oyster saloons, grocery stores and the "gartens" where families and friends met and drank beer could be found around that area. The Atlantic Garden which was a big hall with lots of bars and lunch counters was one of the most famous places of Little Germany and it was always full of people who enjoyed their leisure time there.

The early German immigrants were in high repute among the Americans. These "admired the industriousness, moral values and character of the Germans who replaced the long-vanished New York Dutch as custodians of these solid values" (Homberger, 1998, p.98).

Many Germans worked as manufacturers; they were "tailors, boot and shoemakers, cabinet and piano-makers, cigarmakers, and upholsterers"[5] and the trade union movement of New York was mainly established by the Germans. When industrialization came to the tenements on the Lower East Side in the 1870s the German immigrants looked for better accommodations and moved to Yorkville and Harlem.

Since the 1870s the 10th, 11th, 13th and 17th wards which had mostly been inhabited by Germans or German-Americans, since they provided the immigrants with work in "artisan workshops, shipyards, slaughterhouses and factories"[6], were filled by Jewish immigrants from Eastern Europe (the Ost Juden). And by the turn of the century just a small number of German immigrants remained in this district where once masses of Bavarians, Prussians, and others came together,

---

[5] Homberger, Eric. *The Historical Atlas of New York City.* 1998. p.98
[6] Homberger, Eric. *The Historical Atlas of New York City.* 1998. p.98+99

even though there was always a strong separation between Catholics and Protestants.

When Levinsky in Abraham Cahan's novel *The Rise of David Levinsky* arrives in New York he is out of orientation, until an inhabitant helps him and says: "Walk straight ahead. [...] Just keep walking until you see a lot of Jewish people" (Cahan, 1966, p.92). Levinsky and almost all Jewish immigrants of that time managed to find their way to the Lower East Side which became their new home.

Here one could find kosher butchers, Yiddish theaters, and the stronghold of the pushcart trade which sold almost every available good was at home here. Many of the Jewish immigrants were tailors, shoemakers, carpenters and dressmakers. Hester Street describes the district where the Jewish immigrants found their new home in the city.

Two million Jews from Poland, Russia, Austria-Hungary and the Balkans entered the United States between 1880 and 1920 and most of them decided to settle in New York on the Lower East Side. Their homes were the tenements with mostly five floors and about four extremely small apartments on every storey. Big families with a lot of children and relatives had to share tiny and crowded rooms where hardly one ray of light could find its way trough. Sanitation was bad since there was almost no possibility to get some fresh air into the little chambers, and plumbing was also scarce and just available in very primitive forms. Death and diseases like tuberculosis were the inevitable results; and especially the children died.

Despite these horrible living conditions with which many immigrants were confronted, "Jewish culture and religion flourished" (Homberger, 1998, p.132). Some hundreds of synagogues as well as religious schools were built, religious goods were produced and ritual baths were established. Besides, one could find Yiddish theater companies, literary societies, Yiddish and Hebrew publishers as well as Jewish newspapers.

Jews helped each other by calling groups into life which were responsible to provide people, mostly those who emigrated from the same city, town or village in Europe, with insurance, burial, benefits and cemeteries. These groups were called *landsmenschaften*. Moreover, new arrivals received help from the Hebrew Immigrant Aid Society.

After the 1863 Draft Riots "the southeastern edge of the Village became 'Little Africa,' the principal residential area in New York for African-Americans" (Homberger, 1998, p.134). Soon immigrants from Italy who left the Lower East Side also moved to the area. The Italians brought the cafés and little restaurants to the Village which supplied the area with the distinct charm it still spreads today.

Because of the new arrivals Greenwich Village got its own tenements, and factories also came up very soon. And by the end of the 19th century the area was about to become an industrial slum. This could only be prevented by the upcoming mobility (subway and automobile) of the early 20th century which made many Village factories go bankrupt and suddenly offered a lot of empty and cheap space, mostly rented by artists.

Like the Jews, the Italians had also established a miniaturized version of their home country. Italian banks, shops, newspapers, goods, food, priests and language filled their district. Besides, religious festivals were as common as in "Jewtown".

The Italians were mostly farmers, farm workers or common laborers, usually from the rural areas of south Italy. There were just very few professionals among the new arrivals. America wanted to welcome the ambitious, determined and willing with regard to work and risk taking. In many cases, when success set in for the immigrants, they left their quarters to find a home in a better area.

Throughout the years, decades and almost two centuries of immigration to the city, a movement of the different ethnic groups had taken place until they were spread all over the metropolis. Places left by older immigrants were inhabited by newly arrived ones, changing the face of the city continuously. After a while, many of the immigrants completely assimilated to the American system and totally cut with the past and the roots of their culture.

Masses of Jewish and Italian immigrants started their new American life in the slums once inhabited by the German and Irish immigrants. Today, there are Chinatowns in Lower Manhattan, Brooklyn and Queens. Koreans have established a little Seoul in Flushing Queens with Korean stores, churches, food and the Korean language spoken. In Washington Heights immigrants from the Dominican

Republic created their own territory on the island with its own city structure and own commercial and social life.

Even though ethnic districts are still in existence, many immigrants share distinct quarters with all kinds of nationalities and ethnic groups where their origin does not belong to the prevailing group. Therefore one can find many poly-ethnic neighborhoods in New York City, mainly inhabited by immigrants of a small number like in Elmhurst.

Ethnic communities have the positive aspects of help, support, social and cultural bonds, understanding as well as identification. However, they also offer fewer opportunities to enter better schools and colleges outside the ghetto. Besides, they are often a barrier to the integration into the advantages, comforts and facilities of the urban life.

> The time has come when every American citizen [...] must regard with grave misgiving the mighty tide of immigration that, unless something is done, will soon poison or at least pollute the very fountainhead of American life and progress. Big as we are [...] we cannot safely swallow such an endless-course dinner [...] without getting indigestion and perhaps

national appendicitis. (Frank P. Sargent, Commissioner General of Immigration at Ellis Island, January 1905. (In Homberger, 1998, p.137)

For many immigrants integration into the new country with its different values and customs was not easy. For a lot of them it meant a lot of problems. Moreover, the newcomers were often confronted with racial, cultural and ethnic discrimination.

The topic of discrimination, hatred and prejudice against the immigrants is also present in Dos Passos' novel *Manhattan Transfer*. This general negative attitude towards them is for example expressed in the following paragraph:

> 'No I tell you, Wilkinson, New York is no longer what it used to be [...] City's overrun with kikes and low Irish, that's what's the matter with it. [...] I tell you the Catholics and the Jews are going to run us out of our own country, that's what they are going to do.' 'It's the new Jerusalem,' put in Aunt Emily laughing. 'It's no laughing matter; when a man's worked hard all his life to build up a business and that sort of thing he dont want to be run out by a lot of damn foreigners, does he Wilkinson?' (Dos Passos, 1953, p.101)

Racial and ethnic prejudices were highly present in the 19th and early 20th century during the first big immigration waves. But even today the problem is still in existence. People like Madison Grant, the founder of the New York Zoological Society, editors of popular and influential newspapers like the *New York Times* or the *Saturday Evening Post*, as well as the social reformer and author Jacob A. Riis were influenced by racial stereotypes and made generalizing, often insulting and discriminating comments and remarks about the diverse immigrants like the Jews, Italians or the Chinese.

Riis entitles the Italian as a "born gambler" and he describes the Jewish immigrants the following way: "Thrift is the watchword of Jewtown [...] at once its strength and its fatal weakness, its cardinal virtue and its foul disgrace. [...] Life itself is of little value compared with even the leanest bank account. In no other spot does life wear so intensely bald and materialistic an aspect as in Ludlow Street" (Riis, 1971, p.86).

Some politicians also supported racial discrimination to fight and reduce immigration with the help of the public opinion. They tried to persuade the society that these people were inferior races. Finally, in 1924, those who fought the mass influx had achieved their goal when the huge immigration waves from Southern and Eastern Europe were eventually stopped.

There were posters saying: "No Jews or Dogs Admitted Here" (Foner, 2000, p.148). Italians and Eastern European Jews were not regarded as "white" and stereotypes like the "typical Jewish nose" spread. The Africans, Hispanics and other colored people were discriminated against because of their skin color which made them easily identifiable. Thinking "black and white" is still present in our contemporary society, even though it is not spoken out loud in most cases and although all people have the same rights nowadays.

Almost no restrictions to immigration existed until the 1920s. Only people who had contagious diseases or radical and antagonistic political attitudes were not allowed to pass Ellis Island. Besides physically or mentally ill people, criminals and prostitutes were also forbidden to enter the country. Later on immigration authorities blacklisted illiterate people.

However, there were quite a few unwelcomed people who still managed to settle in New York and live there illegally. Like people from China, for example, who entered the country regardless of the Chinese Exclusion Act of 1882. When the Supreme Court allowed children of Chinese-Americans to become American citizens and come to the United States, so-called "paper sons" evolved. Those were people who bought papers for legal immigration from Chinese-Americans that told the government that they had a child in China even though this was a lie.

In the 1920s immigration restriction laws evolved with the "Quota-Act" from 1921 and the "Immigration-Act" of 1924 which stopped the great influx of immigrants all at once. Soon much less people from Italy, Poland and Russia arrived. However, the numbers of the so-called "old" immigrants like Germans, Britons and the Irish ascended. The city started to become "less foreign".

However, it were "immigrants, and especially the children of immigrants [who] played a crucial role in establishing the supremacy of New York" (Homberger, 1998, p.119). Famous and successful people like George Gershwin, Fiorello La

Guardia, Arthur Miller, Lee Strasberg or Andy Warhol, to name just a few of those who made it, verify this.

People had entered the United States from all over the world to experience their own "from rags to riches"-story. And even though hundreds of thousand people had to start with nothing in the land of unlimited possibilities and were forced to live under inhuman circumstances, there was always the hope to get out of the gutter one day and swim with the big fish. The fairy tale of "the new man created by the New World"[7] could sometimes really become true and gave hope to millions.

As for the American Dream, it can only be realized through hard work. The famous self-made man fulfilled his dream with much effort. The slogan was always the same: "You can be whatever you want to be, if you only work hard enough and never give up." The father of Mike Gold, who is the author of *Jews Without Money* (1930), put it like this: "I came to understand it was not a land of fun. It was a land of Hurry-Up. There was no gold to be dug in the streets here. Derbies were not fun-hats for holidays. They were work-hats.

---

[7] Homberger, Eric. *The Historical Atlas of New York City.* 1998. p.119

Nu, so I worked! With my hands, my liver and sides! I worked" (in Homberger, 1998, p.120)!

A more natural phrasing in 21st-century English would be: "He who does not love wine, wife, and song will be a fool his whole life long." A print published by Kimmel and Voigt in New York, 1873. In addition to its obvious meaning (and a reference to Strauss' "Wine Wife and Song Waltz"), this is also a vigorous assertion of the cultural values of German-American immigrants in the face of "Temperance" and "Maine Law" campaigners (i.e. alcohol prohibitionists), and other reformers who judged immigrants from a "native American" and/or English-speaking Protestant fundamentalist point of view. Library of Congress.

V.   Melting Pot or Salad Bowl: The Ambiguity of the Immigrants' Identity

> 'Weren't the Pilgrim fathers immigrants two hundred years ago?' She took from her desk a book called 'Our America,' by Waldo Frank, and read to me: 'We go forth all to seek America. And in the seeking we create her. In the quality of our search shall be the nature of the America that we create.' [...] Through my inarticulate groping and reaching-out I had found the soul – the spirit – of America! (Yezierska, 1991, p.127)

Immigrants often represent an ambiguous, poly-national, multicultural, sometimes paradox and contradicting attitude and way of living. They have cultural, familial, religious, economic and political bonds to their native society and ethnic group, as well as ties to their new home country connected with the adaptation to the values and habits of the American society.

A deep relation to their roots is often still in existence because of pride, patriotism, a longing for identification, strength within the group, feeling of community, or out of sentimental or familial reasons when there are still relatives living in the Old World.

Several immigrants, especially the Italians, used to be so-called "transmigrants". They had established their home in two different worlds, one in the new and one in the old one. The bonds with their former home country were so tight that the problems of lacking acceptance and having no security in the United States connected them closer with Italy. Therefore many Italians worked in America and returned year by year to their mother country to live from the money they had earned in America. Many of them bought a piece of land or a house back in Europe.

These "transnational households" were families which were torn apart and lived in two different countries then. At the end of the 19th and beginning of the 20th century almost 80 percent of the Italian immigrants were men. Their wives, children, and parents were still in Italy and waited for their husbands, fathers, and sons to send them money and eventually a ticket so that they could follow them. This behavior or rite was also true for many Jews who came to the U.S. alone and sent for their families several months, however, in most cases, several years later.

The historic figure and famous immigrant writer Anzia Yezierska experienced this kind of chain migration herself. She and the rest of her family were brought to the U.S. by the money of one of her brothers who had come to the States a couple of years in advance.

A similar kind of immigration is described in Abraham Cahan's novelette *Yekl* where the protagonist Jake behaves just like almost every male Jewish immigrant who had left his family behind. Like a daily routine he sends letters and money back to his wife who is still in Russia.

But this was not the only way money came back to the Old World. Aid organizations in the New World like the Jewish *landsmanshaftn* or other associations collected money, often on benefit activities and events, to support their home country. This way millions of dollars crossed the ocean several times. Immigrants of the first generation were often at home in two societies.

Some of the transnational immigrants even returned to their home country forever. As already mentioned, this behavior was mostly true for the Italians. However, there were also quite a number of Jews who returned to Russia at the end of the 19th century. For many Italians, America became "their workshop". They acted just like the Italian ice-cream café owners in Germany who return to Italy when the season is over. Seasonal work in America was quite normal for the immigrants; sometimes they were several weeks without work during which they often returned back home.

The U.S. had a great interest in Americanizing the immigrants to keep the money as well as the cheap work forces in the own country. Besides, assimilation should help to secure the American society and its values.

Today it is easier for the immigrants to keep in touch with their home country since there are planes, telephones and the internet which make facile communication possible. The internationalizing character of the mass media enables people all over the world to regard themselves as cosmopolitans.

Because of the mass media and the deep and worldwide impact and presence of American popular culture it is easier for the immigrants to adapt to the American society since they are already used to it. However, even though there are fewer barriers between people and cultures nowadays, there are still many opposing and contradicting systems, values, opinions and attitudes on this earth which prevent this world from living in harmony and perfect understanding.

There have always been two diverse points of view with regard to the question Michele Guillaume Jean de Crèvecoeur, a wealthy farmer who found his new home in the Hudson River Valley, asked in his *Letters from an American Farmer*, in 1782: "What then is the American, this new man" (in Lang, 1988, p.139)?

The answer he found was already described by Tom Paine, another European emigrant who had entered the States just a short time in advance. In 1776 Paine published a famous revolutionary pamphlet with the title *Common Sense* in which he made the statement "that the American were not transplanted Englishmen. They were a mixture of many European peoples, a nation of immigrants" (in Higham, 1984, p.3).

However, the opinion that all Americans, besides the Native Americans, once came to this land as immigrants was not shared by the majority during Crèvecoeur's and Paine's time. A lot of people had and still have the same idea of an

American as John Jay had and put it: "One united people – a people descended from the same ancestors, speaking the same language, professing the same religion, attached to the same principles of government, very similar in their manners and customs" (in Higham, 1984, p.3). And today there are still several writers who talk of America "not as an eclectic and cosmopolitan society, but as the creation of one dominating group" (Higham, 1984, p.3/4).

This way one can define a certain ambiguity in the identity of an American. On the one hand there is the idea of a unified society with the melting pot as one of its most powerful symbols and representatives, and on the other hand one has a vision of persistent separateness of a society which is split up in some basic sense. And it is this "unity versus diversity"-problem which not only describes the origins and character of the American people, but which also defines the conflict the immigrants of the 19th and 20th century had to deal with. And this is also present in the lives of contemporary immigrants.

Captured between the "celebration of the incorruptible autonomy of the ethnic group [and the] idea of a national culture"[8], between patriotism and the melting pot, these people often had problems in defining their identity and sometimes they never found it. "Diversity and homogeneity intertwine so densely in [the] American experience"[9] that many people are distorted within themselves and are not able to decide for one of the opposite ways. In this process of seeking for an own identity many of the searchers lose themselves or get lost on the way.

As mentioned above (in the course of chapter IV), the freshly arrived immigrants were mostly confronted with a certain rootlessness after they had left behind their old life and entered a new and strange world which had often nothing in common with their home country. They had to adapt to a new system, new customs and values and often they did not know how to speak the language.

Therefore, many immigrants of the first generation tried to stick to their old traditions and to their own community to get a feeling of being at home. They wanted to avoid getting lost in the new and unknown place which was crowded with all kinds of identities, nationalities and ethnic groups and

---

[8] Higham, John. *Send These to Me – Immigrants in Urban America*. 1984. p.xii
[9] Higham, John. *Send These to Me – Immigrants in Urban America*. 1984. p.4

where one could easily lose track of things. And so they clang together in their own ethnic quarters where they lived with hundreds or thousands of other immigrants having the same ethnic background. Here they kept to their traditions and values to have a sense of identity at least.

And even though they minded their own business and kept parts of their former home alive, "they were not less truly New Yorkers for going directly about their business single-mindedly, amidst a profusion of confessional, regional and voluntary associations, lodges, fellowships and clubs which they summoned into existence" (Homberger, 1998, p.94). Like gentlemen from the old and aristocratic New York who had their clubs on Fifth Avenue, the immigrants had founded their own societies on the city's Lower East Side.

In 1892 there were already 136 religious communities, and by 1914 the number of benevolent communities in the same part of the town had risen up to 534, theoretically having a place for every immigrant family. "These communities – the embodiment of the Two Nations which made up New York – brought their histories, their stories, to the city" (Homberger, 1998, p.94).

The first writers among the immigrants often experienced the assimilation of greenhorns as a rather negative process which was unavoidable and often dreadful. Later on, during the last decades of the 19th century this opinion developed into a positive view when authors described amalgamation as something good and pleasing for the immigrants. "The figure of the alien who eventually adopted the values of the New World, suffering from the discrepancy of the value-systems of his native and adopted home country, became a topos in literature" (Lang, 1988, p.140).

However, there are also quite a few examples of immigrants who immediately adapted to their new home and who could not wait to take over the American way of life.

In his short story *Yekl* from 1896 Abraham Cahan's hero Jake wants to get rid of his immigration image as soon as possible. He wants to be a part of America and the American way of life and he takes it on with every single aspect of it, not sparing out immoralities and vulgarity. The former pious Jew loses his religious roots, becomes a playboy and gambler and is not able to live with his wife anymore after her arrival a couple of years after his immigration. Jake who calls himself "a real American" cannot and also does not want to go back to his old life. His opinion becomes clear when one hears him say: "Once I live in America I want to know that I live in America. *Dot'sh a' kin' a man I am*! One must not be a *greenhorn*. Here a Jew is as good as a Gentile" (Cahan, 1970, p.5).

Cahan who lived on the Lower East Side and was an immigrant himself did not see his protagonist Jake in an all too tragic light. He described Jake's change of character as a "whimsical transformation", something that happened to many thousands of immigrants. To make room for assimilation and Americanization one had to give up the Old World with all its traditions, values and customs and therefore Jake was not the exception among the masses of immigrants.

Abraham Cahan was born in 1860 in Padberberezer, a village close to the Lithuanian town Vilna. His family was highly religious and Cahan should become a rabbi. However, he chose the teacher profession and became politically involved. Because of his active support of the Russian rebels, Cahan had to flee the country. He emigrated to New York at the end of the 19th century, respectively in 1882. He was a young Russian Jewish intellectual who rebelled against the tyrannical system in his home country, being inspired by the social philosophers of Russia as well as the revolutionary underground organizations.

Among these rebels who included other immigrant writers such as Mary Antin, the author of *The Promised Land,* Abraham Cahan was one of the most notable and important personalities. One cannot reduce him to a single profession or field of activity, since he played a major role as a teacher, a developer and originator of the huge American labor movement, as an orator, a journalist, a novelist and the editor of the most widespread and read Yiddish newspaper in the world, the *Jewish Daily Forward.*

When Abraham Cahan came to the U.S. he first started out in the sweatshops of the ghetto where he finally got involved into the labor movement and Socialist activities. He became a journalist for a Socialist Jewish newspaper and eventually he started his editor career with the popular and widely known *Jewish Daily Forward* which he co-founded in 1897 and of which he was the editor for a period of over 50 years until he died in 1951.

One of his first published works was the novelette *Yekl – A Tale of the New York Ghetto* which he wrote in 1896. Even though this short novel did not get the high reputation it probably deserved, *Yekl* is an important contribution to immigrant fiction. It focusses on the process of assimilation and Americanization which goes along with the problem of estrangement. Jake, formerly known as Yekl emigrated to New York alone. Like many men at that time Jake, which is the American name he received at his arrival on Ellis Island, came to the country to earn enough money so that his family, namely his wife and son would be able to follow him to the States after a certain while.

Historically, there were much more immigrant men than women in the city; fathers, brothers and sons who tried so set up a living and enable their relatives to join them. Men came to the New World to earn money which they partly sent back home to their wives, children and other relatives until those could finally come to America themselves. In fact, it often took several months and usually even years until the other members of the family could finally sail over to the Promised Land to reunite with their husbands, brothers and fathers.

Jake, too, sends money and finally the tickets back home to his wife who is eventually able to come to the United States after three long years of separation from her husband. The reunion of the couple and their son seems to be impossible from the very beginning since two diverging worlds collide. Jake, who had sent the money more out of an automatic behavior which almost everyone did and which became part of his everyday life, is shocked when he is confronted with his wife who still incorporates the Old World he left behind. Gitl expresses everything he tried to abandon, this rural and deeply religious image which lacks any kind of big city flair and lady chic. Now, as they stand face to face he cannot feel anything but disgust.

This difficulty of reunion, when the Old World, incorporated by the new arrivals, finally met the new one, embodied by the older and assimilated immigrants who had already gone through a huge part of the Americanization process, was a general problem at that time and historically happened to many immigrants. After several months, in many cases even years, apart from each other former couples and families met again as strangers which were often unable to deal with one another.

Divorce was sometimes the only solution to this problem which the protagonist Jake and his wife Gitl also face in Cahan's novel. The estrangement of the couple had taken place during the time of separation and while Gitl is still the religious and loving housewife without glamour, Jake had turned into an Americanized "Yankee", as he likes to call himself. He is a charmer and playboy who loves going to the dancing school with Mamie, Fannie, and Beckie. He had lost his deeply religious attitude on the way and learned to enjoy his regained bachelorhood. Now, being accustomed to perfumed and dressed up Jewish-American women, he cannot stand the smell and looks of the Old World, the rural atmosphere, and the traditional lifestyle anymore which his wife brings along.

From the day of her arrival he wishes that she would have never arrived in New York and he hates her as soon as he sees her face. Instead, Jake feels affection for his dancing school companion Mamie and it only takes a short time until he is not able to hide his disgust and hatred towards his "greenhornlike" wife anymore. And even though Gitl tries to arouse the interest and admiration of her husband with all possible means – she even gets herself a new look – Jake isn't impressed at all. The newcomer doesn't have a single chance to gain back her assimilated husband who had fallen for the Americanized Mamie.

However, it is not only the Old World which is brought back into Yekl's life through his wife. Having a wife and a son at home has also taken away all the bachelor freedom he used to enjoy over three years. Jake continues to go out whenever he wants to without letting his wife know where he is about to go. "Gitl was used to his goings and comings without explanation" (Cahan, 1970, p.58).

Yosselé, the son of Gitl and Jake stands in between. On the one hand he is a newcomer who is deeply connected with his mother. On the other hand he immediately receives an American name like his father. Yosselé turns into Joey like it was the case for many immigrants who got American names at their arrival on Ellis Island. However, not everyone decided to keep his or her new assimilated name, and Jake's wife who remains Gitl throughout the novel is a perfect example for that.

In this story not only the names but also the clothes reflect the way of life of the protagonists. Gitl therefore stands for the freshly arrived immigrant who is still closely connected with her home country and the traditions and values lived by its people. Jake, however, incorporates the newly born American who cuts his bonds with the past and a world he had left behind. Joey, the child who falls between two stools, is neither a representative of the Old, nor a member of the New World. However, he will sooner or later become an assimilated immigrant.

The two different worlds are also portrayed and symbolized in the language which is often a mixture of English and Yiddish. This is also a sign that assimilation has not reached its perfection yet.

In the end Jake and Gitl are getting divorced. At that time the protagonist has already promised Mamie to marry her directly after he is free again. On the day of the divorce Gitl has finally lost "the rustic, 'greenhornlike' expression [...] from her face and manner"[10]. She has turned into a much more self-confident, assimilated and an Americanized woman. And even though it wasn't her wish to get divorced from Yekl and she weeps desperately afterwards, deeply inside of her she knows that she will be the victorious in the end: "At the bottom of her heart she felt herself far from

---

[10] Cahan, Abraham. *Yekl – A Tale of the New York Ghetto.* 1970. p.83

desolate, being conscious of the existence of a man who was to take care of her and her child [...]. Already on her way from the rabbi's house, while her soul was full of Jake and the Polish girl, there had fluttered through her imagination a picture of the grocery business which she and Bernstein were to start with the money paid to her by Jake" (Cahan, 1970, p.88/89).

Jake, however, who is on the way to his wedding with Mamie, becomes aware of the fact that he is not free at all now. His firstly "hilarious mood" due to the feeling that "a great burden" has "rolled off his heart" and his loving affection and passion for Mamie, the Polish girl, soon cease when he has to realize that he hasn't gained back his bachelorhood.[11] "He was painfully reluctant to part with his long-coveted freedom so soon after it had at last been attained, and before he had had time to relish it" (Cahan, 1970, p.89).

Jake becomes aware of Gitl's triumph over him and that he had lost his liberty, family and money and won a new marriage which now appears to him as an inescapable prison. The "violent lurch" he feels in his heart at the end describes his desperate feeling of being captured, and the way to the

---

[11] Cahan, Abraham. *Yekl – A Tale of the New York Ghetto.* 1970. p.89

mayor who shall marry Mamie and Jake is comparable to Yekl's way to the scaffold. His future appears to him as "dark and impenetrable". Jake's American way of life, as he had lived it for more than three years, comes to an end.

For some of the immigrants the picture they had in mind of a typical American was rather like a myth which had spread among them. Many of the new arrivals expected streets paved with gold and the most beautiful landscape comparable to paradise. Jacob A. Riis, in his book *The Making of an American*, notes down the words of an immigrant who arrives in New York in 1870 and believes that the whole country has the same rules and customs everywhere:

> So as properly to make my own place in the procession ... as I conceived the custom of the country to be, I made it my first business to buy a navy revolver of the largest size, investing in the purchase exactly one-half of my capital. I strapped the weapon on the outside of my coat and strode up Broadway, conscious that I was following the fashion of the country. I knew it upon the authority of a man who had been there before me and had returned, a gold digger in the early days of

California ... (in Homberger, 1998, p.95)

The problem of wanting to become a part of the new, but being deeply rooted in the old often evokes the problem that one does belong to none of each side. For those who faced this destructive ambiguity which means that one is not able to involve parts of one world into the other, it often meant that they were finally thrown out of both worlds.

Within the quarters the traditions of the Old World, the customs and values of their former lives came up again and they were willingly or unwillingly captured between two worlds again. Especially for those immigrants of the first generation these problems occurred and most of them did not find their way out of the ambiguity throughout their life. And sometimes they totally lost their identity on the way.

"It was the collective memories of the assimilated [...] which created the strongly ethnic neighborhoods of the city and which gave a particular fervor to the celebration of traditional saints' days in Little Italy, and shaped the patriotic joy in "Kleindeutschland" when the Prussian army defeated the French at the battle of Sedan in 1870" (Homberger, 1998, p.95). And today these patriotic traditions are still present in colorful and huge parades on

Fifth Avenue like the Irish St. Patrick's Day, the national holiday of the green island.

Anzia Yezierska originated from an area called the Pale, which was the Jewish ghetto between Russia and Poland. For many people who had to live there the first problems of identification occurred in this district since some people identified themselves with Poland and others claimed to be Russian. The Lower East Side in New York often meant continuity with regard to poverty, oppression and the problem of identification for many immigrants.

In *Red Ribbon on a White Horse*, Yezierska's semi-fictional autobiography which was published in 1950, the authoress talks about the conflicts in a Jewish community and the struggle for identity in a new home country which went along with the fine bonds that connected the immigrants with the "Anglo-Saxon Christian majority". Getting out of the ghetto and becoming successful in the American society through hard work and under horrible conditions, is one of the main issues of this book.

Yezierska was born in the 1880s and emigrated to New York around 1890, together with her family. She was the youngest of eight children of a Jewish family with a highly religious father and a passive mother. When the family entered the New World, Anzia's brother, who had come to the States a couple of years before, had already organized a new home for them: a tenement flat on the Lower East Side.

The authoress and her family were poor people, and throughout her life Yezierska "saw herself standing on the street with her nose pressed against the bakery window: hungry and shut out. [...] Not belonging became her identity, and then her subject" (Vivian Gornick in Yezierska, 1991, p.vii).

Yezierska became a writer and she published several novels and story collections dealing with her immigrant background and the problem of being "poverty-stricken and socially outcast" (in Yezierska, 1991, p.vii). This book discusses five of her publications on the immigration topic, namely *Bread Givers, How I found America, Hungry Hearts & Other Stories, Red Ribbon on a White Horse* and *Salome of the Tenements.*

Anzia was different from the other women in her family. While her sisters worked in sweatshops, married early and imitated her mother, she was the rebel, the restless soul, the powerful and intelligent mind filled with passion as well as anger and frustration.

For Yezierska, as for many other Jews, success was deeply connected with education. Although she worked hard all day long, she educated herself at night school, managed it to take courses at Columbia University and persuaded the professor John Dewey to integrate her into his seminar and his projects. However, even though she became famous, rich and successful due to her writing, and although she wrote screenplays for Hollywood movies in California, Yezierska "remained [...] lost and angry and forlorn [...], gasping for breath" (in Yezierska, 1991, p.viii).

Through her radical and rebellious breakout of her traditional family life and the poverty and dirt of the Lower East Side, the roots she tried to cut became even stronger. A paradox attitude evolved which denied and hated the past and all the oppressive and degrading aspects of it, and which loved it at the same time with all the colorful and lively atmosphere of the community, the deep connection between the people, the emotional and passionate character, and sentimental traditions. "Her rise out of poverty and oppression reflected the economic rise of many Jews, but like other authors of the time [Abraham Cahan for example], she was never able to separate herself from those who were unable to break out of the ghetto" (Gay Wilentz in Yezierska, 1995, p.x/xi).

Later on Yezierska worked at the settlement houses herself, the charity organizations she criticizes in *Salome of the Tenements*. Even though she did not have a high opinion of those organizations she needed this job to raise her daughter as a single mother. She told her friend Rose Pastor Stokes: "I see how the people are crushed and bled and spat upon in the process of getting charity and I must keep my mouth shut or lose my job" (in Yezierska, 1995, p.xi). She became rich overnight, getting $10,000 and a monthly wage of $200. But she always felt unable to write away from the Lower East Side which was her inspiration. Yezierska died in 1970 and maintained a writer until the end.

Back in the 1920s Anzia Yezierska was well known, not only among the intellectual immigrant writers but among the people in general. Her novels and short stories about Jewish immigrant life, poverty and dirt, in a yet colorful community of the Lower East Side, made her famous.

Bread Givers which was published in 1925 is one of her most famous and also most autobiographical novels. The story deals with the "struggle between a father of the Old World and a daughter of the New". It tells of the ambiguous character of first generation immigrants who are in fact often captured between two worlds, equally hating and loving the old system, and trying to escape, only to find an even stronger way back.

Most of Yezierska's writing can be called semi-biographical or semi-fictional since the authoress usually treats her own experiences in her novels and short stories. She often uses the topics of Americanization, escape from the old traditions and deeply rooted religious living and attitude, an urge for education, emancipation, freedom and equality, a longing for love with a self-chosen lover (something that was impossible in Europe, where marriages were traditionally organized by the heads of a couple's families), and the vision to realize the hope and dreams she has had of America before her arrival.

Yezierska herself was a rebel who fought against the strict Jewish traditions lived and embodied by her father - like the protagonist of *Bread Givers* does. However, when the girl of the novel has finally made it and has become an assimilated member of the American society as a teacher, engaged with an American, she finally finds her way back to her roots, her loving family and her father. Eventually, she ends up as a representative of both worlds - emotionally belonging to the old one, however, socially and economically being an American.

The settlement programs as well as the love and marriage, respectively the intermarriage of Rose and Graham Stokes, form the historical background for Anzia Yezierska's first novel *Salome of the Tenements* which was published in 1923. This theme is expressed by the husband of the loving couple of the book, "John Manning, the upper-class, native-born Protestant American", when he asks his bride Sonya who is a poor Jewish immigrant: "Are we not the mingling of the races? The oriental mystery and the Anglo-Saxon clarity that will pioneer a new race of men" (Yezierska, 1995, p.108)?

The novel criticizes the settlement education projects which were established for the poor immigrants to become Americanized and be transformed into an assimilated member of the dominant American society. The melting pot theory which assumed that all immigrants can be turned into Americans when the right steps are taken forms the basis of these settlements. The differences between the predominant Anglo-Saxon culture and the diverse, often European new arrivals (in Yezierska's case Jewish immigrants from Eastern Europe) should be abolished in favor of the prevailing group.

Besides criticizing the hypocrisy of the reformers and 'selfless saints' of the settlements the novel also faces the problematic aspects of marriage between different classes, cultures, races and ethnic groups. Moreover, it expresses critique towards the upper society whose members come to the Lower East Side to offer their help to the poor immigrants but doing it out of selfishness, since they are afraid of the overtaking power of other cultures than their own. Furthermore, they ignore the horrible circumstances of the poor in New York City's slums by idolizing poverty as a nobility and purely natural style, and by insisting on their privileged status.

Yezierska involves her own life and work, the upcoming of settlement houses at the end of the 19th and beginning of the 20th century, the famous story of her close friend Rose

Pastor who married the millionaire and philanthropist Graham Stokes, and her own class exceeding relationship with the University professor and settlement establisher John Dewey into her book *Salome of the Tenements.*

Rose Pastor was a writer and labor activist. She worked in sweatshops like Yezierska and the two Jewish intellectuals were very close friends. The two women had much in common. They were both poor Jewish immigrants who lived in the tenements of the Lower East Side and who both tried to escape their old life by intermingling with "real" Americans of high status. The two writers experienced a similar kind of class-crossing love story, which helped them to escape their milieu and which supported them in becoming successful.

However, both women got disappointed by their Anglo-Saxon knights on their fake white horses. Rose Pastor was often regarded as "the luckiest girl in America." Yezierska had the opinion that her friend was going to "make history" since she was a symbol for the fusion of the rich and poor as well as Christians and Jews. Anzia herself yearned for a "physical and emotional" way out of the East Side ghetto, but she could not eliminate the thought that she would betray her people, her culture and her traditions if she left this part of her life behind without looking back.

John Dewey who supported her writing and with whom the authoress had a short but passionate relationship, and Graham Pastor Stokes, the millionaire, socialist and philanthropist who realized a fairy-tale American Dream by marrying Rose Pastor, both influenced the novel *Salome of the Tenements* since they both functioned as a model for the rich and Anglo-Saxon protagonist John Manning. Like the two social reformers, this upper class representative also works as an activist in the establishment of the settlements.

Here he finally meets Sonya, the Jewish immigrant factory worker who immediately wants to catch the millionaire to marry her way out of the ghetto. Sonya Vrunsky, the female protagonist of the novel is created out of Yezierska's soul and character, but she lives Rose Pastor's life. She knows, to get ahead in America one does not only have to work hard but also needs to find out who has the power in this country. Making this person one's husband is one possibility to climb up the social and economic ladder faster than other people. Like other immigrant women Sonya visited settlement programs to get a possibility to flee the ghetto, hopefully by marrying a rich reformer.

Education and assimilation were definitely not their (only) ambitions: "'To think how I once hated settlements. ...Where else can a poor girl like me meet her millionaire if not in the settlement?' Sonya rationalized her inconsistency. 'How did Rose Pastor catch on to Graham Stokes'" (Yezierska, 1995, p.82/83)? Yezierska uses Rose's name to make the distinction clear between her personal friend and her fictional character Sonya and to remind the reader of Rose's story.

Like the biblical figure Salome Sonya falls back on illusion to get the man of her dreams. Sonya's illusion is created by impressing Manning with fake images. She organizes herself a new dress from Jaky Solomon, a friend and later fiancé of hers and she borrowed $100 to style her rotten tenement apartment so that it looked cozy instead of filthy. Manning is impressed by this manipulation which he takes for the truth. He celebrates poverty as something noble: "Why, it's the glory of poverty that it enforces simplicity! ...The thing that appeals to me so much about the East Side...is their directness, their unscheming naturalness" (Yezierska, 1995, p.73).

Sonya realizes that the settlement house of her husband cannot be differentiated from those charity organizations she knew when she was a child. They were "designed to keep people poor and grateful for the little they get" (in Yezierska, 1995, p.xx). Manning ignores Sonya's critique: "Tell me in plain words how can there be democratic understanding between those who are free to walk into steerage and the steerage people who are not allowed to give one step up to the upper deck" (Yezierska, 1995, p.120)?

The ghetto tailor Jaky Solomon, who turns into the famous and successful designer Jacques Hollins, represents the assimilated immigrant who made it in the New World. He is the person standing in between Sonya and John. He comes from the Old World and managed to hop into the world of the Americans through his own hard work. He is the perfect example of the self-made man. However, the change of his name also contributed a lot to his process of Americanization. Hollins "identifies the hypocrisy behind Manning's social reform"[12]: "I suppose [...] playing with poverty is more exciting than knocking golf balls" (Yezierska, 1995, p.30).

---

[12] Wilentz, Gay in Anzia Yezierska. *Salome of the Tenements.* 1995. p.xxii

The novel criticizes "the suffering of the poor or the effects of semi-forced assimilation on social minorities and new immigrants" (Gay Wilentz in Yezierska, 1995, p.xviii).

Liberal reformers like John Dewey and Graham Stokes were a symbol of the America of Anzia's and Rose's dreams, a land where different classes and ethnicities harmonize in their work and personal relationships and create a better America, a land which really fulfills all the hopes of desperate immigrants.

Yezierska wanted to overcome the barriers and oppositions which stood between her and Dewey with regard to ethnicity, culture, race, class and education. However, this bridge could not be built since Anzia's emotionality was confronted with a cold and unemotional culture. Yet, "his rejection reinforced her desire to write" (Gay Wilentz in Yezierska, 1995, p.xiii).

In *Red Ribbon on a White Horse* the authoress says: "In the intoxication of this sudden recognition, all my hunger and longing for love turned to ambition. I saw a place for myself. I saw work. I, the unwanted one, was wanted. If I could not have love, I would have fame, success" (Yezierska, 1950, p.119).

In books like *How I found America* the authoress tries to deal with her life, her immigrant experiences and her inner self. The story "My Own People" which speaks in the third person reflects her own biography:

> Perhaps her family was right in condemning her rashness. Was it worthwhile to give up the peace of home, the security of a regular job – suffer hunger, loneliness, and want – for what? For something she knew in her heart was beyond her reach. Would her writing ever amount to enough to vindicate the uprooting of her past? Would she ever become articulate enough to express beautifully what she saw and felt? What had she, after all, but a stifling, sweatshop experience, a meager, night-school education, and this wild, blind hunger to release the dumbness that choked her? (Yezierska, 1991, p.228)

The tragedy of Anzia Yezierska is that she was never able to free herself from this never-ending hunger for satisfaction during her long life of almost 90 years. Throughout her life she was seeking her own identity, searching for a place where she could find home, rest and inner peace.

However, her childhood experience of being an outcast never stopped teasing her and she suffered from this immigrant background all her life. The authoress tried to free herself through writing, but something inside her told her that she would never be able to find and write the very words which could possibly be the key to her mind-made prison between the Old and New World, between past and future, between restlessness, loneliness, hunger and anger.

"I want to make from myself a person" Yezierska told professor Dewey when she asked him to let her be a part of his seminar and his studies. These words which impressed the professor so much that he allowed her to take part in his course, accompanied Anzia during all the years of her life. With her "wild, blind hunger" she tried to realize these words for herself, but she was trapped in them, as much as she was trapped in her own self, in her own identity, in her immigrant background and her womanhood.

Anzia Yezierska felt guilty throughout her life that her stories about the poor made her rich. Besides, loneliness accompanied her until her death. And this burden she describes in her first book *Hungry Hearts and Other Stories* in the short story *This Is What $10,000 Did to Me*: "Now [...]

I look back and see how happy I ought to have been when I was starving poor, but one of my own people. Now I am cut off by my own for acquiring the few things I have. And those new people with whom I dine and to whom I talk, I do not belong to them. I am alone because I left my own world" (Yezierska, 1991, p.315).

Yezierska is "the girl with her hungry eyes and intense eagerness" which she describes in her short story *Wings*. Here she also mentions that it takes egoism to get ahead: "In America a person can't live on hopes for the next world. In America everybody got to look out for himself" (Yezierska, 1991, p.14). In *Wings* she deals with the urge of an immigrant girl to become an American which can only come true by getting in contact with native-born people: "So you want to be an American! The next step will be to take up some work that will bring you in touch with American people" (Yezierska, 1991, p.25).

The process takes place when the immigrant tries to transform herself from a representative of the Old World to a member of the new one: "I got to have a hat and a new dress. I can't no more wear my 'greenhorn' shawl going out with an American" (Yezierska, 1991, p.17).

Yezierska often repeats the same topics over and over again in her stories and novels. The longing for becoming someone, for getting out of the gutter, for becoming an American fully integrated in the adopted society, the urge for education and the relief felt in writing as well as the paradoxical feeling of guilt and betrayal towards her own people by leaving them behind and getting rich with their story. Being captured between two worlds and imprisoned within her own distorted and passionate self is what the Jewish immigrant writer cannot get rid of throughout her life.

"The immigrant experience is Yezierska's idiom, but the subject is original loss. The bakery against whose window her nose is pressed is not America, it is her own unfrightened self" (in Yezierska, 1991, p.x). And so she says at the end of her autobiography *Red Ribbon on a White Horse*: "With a sudden sense of clarity I realized the battle I thought I was waging against the world had been against myself, against the Jew in me" (Yezierska, 1987, p.212).

With regard to German immigration Caspar Stürenburg (1843-1909) contributed a book to the topic of ethnic communities in urban environments entitled: *Kleindeutschland. Bilder aus dem New Yorker Alltagsleben* which was originally presented in the *New Yorker Staatszeitung*. The book is a collection of several short stories which describe German-American life in the metropolis.

Stürenburg writes about the microcosmical function of the tenements and the living conditions there while using a realistic style of writing which addresses the reader's senses. Besides, the author mentions the mixture of German and English language which affected the inhabitants of the German tenement slums. This was not an exception since the Yiddish language also mingled with English among the Jewish immigrants in their ethnic districts. And so Stürenburg writes: "Unten, der Bierwirth, der eine lease hat und der dieses Umstands viel lieber Erwähnung thut, als er sich an die mortgage seines Brauers auf die saloon-fixtures erinnern läßt..." (in Lang, 1988, p.129).

The author mentions generation conflicts among the German-Americans, ethnic clashes, hard work, poverty, and bad living conditions. However, the American Dream is kept alive throughout the misery of the immigrant experience. The German who comes to America is comparable to a "Hans im Glück" because of his opportunity to find a way out of the ghetto through hard work. Moreover, the writer mentions America's political freedom and open social system. He celebrates the liberty and endless opportunities which are achievable by every hardworking man. However, he also gives a realistic description of the miserable life in the tenement slums and the struggle of German-Americans who suffer to adjust to the American system.

Kathinka Sutro-Schücking (1831-1893), a German authoress who later married and settled in the United States, was a very significant writer with regard to the assimilation process of German immigrants in America. The first novel she writes about the often hard and strenuous adaptation to the new country is called *In Beiden Hemisphären* and was published in 1881.

One of the protagonists in this novel is the aristocrat von Horst who escapes to the United States after he had lost his fortune as well as his honor in Germany. In America he has to experience the hardship of immigrant life by a social decline which brings him in touch with the poor of the new nation. For von Horst the arrival in New York is "the beginning of a descent into hell" (Lang, 1988, p.171). He loses all his material standards as well as his grit while he is desperately searching for a good job, however, with little success. Eventually he gets the opportunity to work as the private secretary of the highly esteemed Jewish banker Ben Ward who himself looks back on an immigrant history: "Glauben Sie wohl, der arme Junge aus der Frankfurter Judengasse wäre heute der einflußreiche, mächtige Ben Ward, eine Geldgröße vor der sich die ganze Welt beugt, wenn er nicht Zähigkeit und Ausdauer besessen hätte" (in Lang, 1988, p.171)?

However, Sutro-Schücking does not only mention the difficult circumstances and the suffering of the immigrants in the New World, she also refers to the positive aspects of emigrating to the U.S. which she believes to be an excellent choice. The problems and difficulties von Horst has to deal with in America resulted from the events and conditions back in Germany. He misses all the opportunities given to him in the New World because he cannot cut off his German past; it is his past which is his only obstacle to become a successful self-made man in America.

In *Eine Liebelose Ehe* Sutro-Schücking deals with assimilation and intermarriage by putting the protagonist, again a German aristocrat, however, an artist who immigrated to New York, into the poor and shabby living conditions of the Bowery. The class-exceeding story sets in when he falls in love with a German-American girl whose father is a self-made man who had realized the American dream for himself and became a millionaire now living among the rich and beautiful people on Fifth Avenue.

The parents of the girl describe two different kinds of assimilation. The father, Mr. William Mertens is characterized as a friendly and enthusiastic man who incorporates the perfect solution of a positive adaptation to the new country with all its rules and values. He had achieved an ideal amalgamation by being aware of his past as well as knowing about his hard work and often miserable times he had to endure until he finally made it. He has not lost his personality and individuality on the way up and most of all "Mr. Mertens successfully harmonizes pride in his German heritage and patriotism for America, thus developing an even stronger personality" (Lang, 1988, p.174).

However, his wife fails to adapt to her Fifth Avenue-life in such an idealized way. She wants to keep her German identity and her social origins secret and is therefore lacking her personality. She gets lost in the process of assimilation by ending up with no identity at all, a person who is not accepted by Germans and Americans alike.

The protagonist himself, the young German artist, has to learn to adopt the values of his future wife on Fifth Avenue. For him this process means a struggle between the principles he does not want to give up and the prosperity awaiting him as his wife's husband. Finally he manages to find a compromise.

"The painful process of adjustment appears as a process of initiation" (Lang, 1988, p.174). Getting introduced to the American system by a mentor, the immigrants eventually find their way out of the slums of the city. When the aristocratic German artist and Mertens' daughter Mathilde, who is already a 100 percent American girl with the ability to speak the German language, finally celebrate their wedding, a positive example of intermarriage takes place which creates a tie between two different nations.

A better social status appears as one positive result of Americanization. However, the immigrants have to give up their old home country's values and its system. Assimilation is a process which prerequisites the "tolerance of all citizens"

(Lang, 1988, p.180). It's not only the immigrants who have to adapt to the American values, it's also the Americans which need to accept the immigrants and let them bring parts of their cultural heritage into their new society which therefore experiences constant progress and change. This would describe the ideal form of adjustment.

In 1894 Sutro-Schücking mentioned the process of adaptation which is ushered by disillusionment and deep roots in the Old World in an additional novel under the title *Dr. Zernowitz*. Zernowitz describes the process himself and the reader experiences different stages in his attitude in the course of the book.

At first he has the opinion that: "Diese Menschen, gewaltsam losgerissen aus dem heimathlichen Boden, meistens zu alt, um leicht ihre Verpflanzung überwinden zu können – waren sämmtlich eben so übel daran wie ich. Auch sie hatten schwer mit dem Dasein zu kämpfen, und vielen stand dabei noch mehr die Unkenntniß der Landessprache hindernd im Weg, wic dei eingefleischte Nativismus der Eingeborenen..." (in Lang, 1988, p.176/77).

Later on his point of view transforms: "...die Stromschnellen des Lebens reißen hin und wieder auch einmal einen recht knorrigen Stamm aus seinem Heimathsboden los und stossen ihn dann so lange unbarmherzig an Fels und Gestein, bis seine rauen Ecken abgeschliffen sind und er glatt und geschmeidig geworden, sich fortan leicht dorthin tragen läßt, wo ihm die gesellschaftlichen Verhältnisse sein Bett bereitet haben" (in Lang, 1988, p.178).

And so Lang states with regard to assimilation: "Over time, the perspective shifts from the authors' emphasis on ethnic, cultural and social distinctions between German immigrants and American natives to the emphasis on underlying similarities and common goals" (Lang, 1988, p.224).

No matter which century or decade we take as a basis, the general problem always remains the same: The process of assimilation often means a barrier accompanied with trouble and difficulties for the older-aged immigrants who are too much established in their old values and traditions and who cannot adapt to the new system as easily as their children or the second generation can do.

Many immigrant mothers who come to the new country and are forced to stay at home to take care for the household and the children have to get taught in the English language by their own infants and often they have to take their siblings with them, any time they are confronted with the American life outside of the ghetto.

In *The Rise of David Levinsky* Abraham Cahan deals with the Americanization of the immigrant. The novel is about a young man who is displaced from his traditional Jewish society and turns into "a restlessly driven individualist" (Higham, 1998, p.83).

With regard to the interpretation of the novel one faces a twofold opinion. On the one hand one can regard Levinsky as an example for the progress of the immigrant, a man who leaves his past behind to assimilate to the New World of which he has become a part. Levinsky would therefore be the personification of the process of Americanization. On the other hand one can also experience the novel as a story of disintegration. Levinsky turns into a person who has lost his roots and is determined to look for new ones throughout his life. A certain loss of identity goes along with this story which has quite a lot of similarities with the semi-autobiographical novels and stories of Anzia Yezierska.

The "rise" of the protagonist David Levinsky is simultaneously a fall which means that both ways of interpretation are true and cannot be regarded apart from each other. Ending up empty with regard to his identity is one of the main statements Cahan expresses with his novel. The protagonist is perfectly able to deal with the change that comes along during the process of coming to America and becoming an American citizen. However, true and deeply emotional relationships that last for a long time become impossible for him to bear.

Western values attracted Levinsky already back in Europe when he was confronted with people who had romantic relationships or were married with a woman they actually loved. For Levinsky Americanization had already found its beginning in the Old World. However, in America the protagonist is faced with an upcoming desire for the great American success story which brings along prosperity from certain businesses. In this process he eventually loses his cultural dream and yearning. "The path of commercial achievement ended in spiritual loss and emptiness"

(Higham, 1984, p.84). Cahan ends the novel with the words of Levinsky who finally realizes where he belongs: "David, the poor lad swinging over a Talmud volume at the Preacher's Synagogue, seems to have more in common with my inner identity than David Levinsky, the well-known cloak-manufacturer" (Cahan, 1966, p.530).

Looking back from the perspective of a new millennium on almost 200 years of immigration to New York, one can definitely say that a continuous repetition takes place. New York is still the city of immigration and this is certainly not about to stop in the near future. And the problems the newcomers face today are very similar to those of the immigrants who entered the New World in the 19th and early 20th century during the first big immigration waves.

Even though the horrible living conditions with regard to windowless, tiny, dirty, and crowded tenement flats or sweatshops have changed since that time, it is still not always paradise for new arrivals in the Big Apple.

Today, Roosevelt Avenue in Queens is the youngest immigration focus of New York and, with regard to ethnicity, the most colorful street in the world. More than 126 nations crowd in this ten kilometers long mile. And although their lives cross each other, they stay separately within their own ethnic grouping.

The avenue has always been a multicultural area where immigrants started their new life in the New World. Once it used to be inhabited by Jewish, Italian, Irish and German immigrants who have now moved away to a great extent. Nowadays, Roosevelt Avenue has a different, even more multifaceted character.

"The corridor", as this mile, surmounted by the tracks of train no. 7 of the New York Transit line, which rushes over the avenue every two minutes, is called, unites the world within its boarders. Between 52nd and 61st street there are still the Irish, at 69th street one will find the Philippine and Uruguayan area, Indian, Pakistani and Bangladeshi people live at 74th street, Colombia and Ecuador have their Roosevelt home at 82nd street, the 90th street is inhabited by Mexico, Bolivia and Peru, the people from the Dominican Republic and El Salvador live at 111th street and the final station Flushing is the home for immigrants from China, Korea and the Ukraine.

The modern immigrants behave in many aspects like their predecessors. Their new homes and lives in the New World are miniaturized reconstructions of the country they originated from. This way they try to protect themselves against the destructive and hard life waiting for them outside in the world of the big business, the fast and intense lifestyle of the Western world, the city that can spit you out in the gutter, if you are not strong or tough enough to survive and make it there.

The problem of the immigrants' protection of their own little miniature worlds is that they separate and isolate themselves from the other world surrounding them. And it is only during their working hours when they spin thin threads between the diverging worlds. And sometimes this mingling during work can have weird results with a Mexican salesman selling Chinese food in the Hong-Kong-covered market of Flushing or dozens of Chinese people selling Tacos and Tortillas in their own Mexican Fast Food restaurants, even though they would never think of eating the food themselves or being friends with someone of the other ethnic group.

However, the next generation or the children of the immigrants who came to the country when they were still little, adapt to the American way of life within a very short amount of time. They have hardly any problems to assimilate to the new culture they live in. The teachers of the Marino P. Jeantet School which is situated on Roosevelt Avenue and often has classes with children from seven different nations, are over and over again astonished how fast the children take over the American way of living. The alienation of the children from their parents starts with the first day in school and rushes on until one finds totally Americanized children with parents who are stuck in their old systems of values and traditions, unable to keep abreast of their offspring and to assimilate to their new home country.

USA, Neue Staatsbürger bei der Vereidigung. Am Anfang eines jeden Jahres wird ein bestimmter Prozentsatz nach Amerika Eingewanderter zu Staatsbürgern erhoben und vereidigt. Die neuen Staatsbürger bei der Vereidigung im Grossen Saal des Justizgebäudes in New York. Rechts im Bilde der Vereidigungsbeamte, davor der Tisch mit den Beglaubigungsurkunden, welche den neuen Bürgern nach Ihrer Vereidigung überreicht werden. Vereinigte Staaten, 1930. Aktuelle-Bilder-Centrale, Georg Pahl (Bild 102). Bundesarchiv, Bild 102-09390 / CC-BY-SA

Cinderella Story of A Servant Girl

NZIA YEZIERSKA LEAVES POTS AND PANS FOR FAME AND RICHES.

HUNGRY heart. Anzia Yezierska.

Join them and you have the Cinderella-like story of filmdom's newest author.

She was an immigrant girl from Poland. Poor. Unlettered. But ambitious.

Worked in a garment factory. Was a cook. A domestic stranger in a strange land, she was hungry-hearted.

Life to her was as seamy as the inner side of the garments on which she labored, as dark as the skillets she scrubbed.

She set about to feed the craving of her soul. She would write! She would make others happy!

She was more proficient as cook than writer. She earned a scholarship in a domestic science school.

Now her story in her own words:

"Before the term was half over I went to the instructor and said, I had enough of cooking—I want better to write.'

"'Write? Bah! You'll starve to death.'

"'If I can't write in American English, I'll write in immigrant English, but write I must,' I answered."

She went to school at night after long days of toil. Then "Hungry Hearts" was accepted. Fame and success bounded to her.

A dinner was given in her honor recently at the Waldorf-Astoria. Less than two years ago, Anzia Yezierska visited that hotel. She entered then through the dark, underground servants' tunnel.

"I was so down and out I did not have the spunk to ask for work as waitress," she says. "I knew I didn't look good enough for that.

"All I asked was for a job as scullery maid, dishwasher or scrubwoman. And even this was refused me."

Now—she is under contract to Goldwyn. She's out at Culver City assisting in the filming of "Hungry Hearts."

And what it takes to make those pictures realistic, Anzia Yezierska can tell—for they are pictures of Anzia Yezierska's heart.

ANZIA YEZIERSKA, FILMDOM'S NEWEST AUTHOR.

STAR DUST

Marguerite Maxwell, Ziegfeld Follies beauty, makes her film debut in Mildred Harris' "Playthings of Desire."

Betty Ross Clarke, who appears in Arbuckle comedies, lived on an Indian reservation in North Dakota when a little girl. She later was a "Russian" dancer in vaudeville.

Bessie Love is to have an important role in Dickens' "Old Curiosity Shop," which is to be filmed in London this spring.

Elliott Dexter has the lead in "The Witching Hour."

Buster Keaton got his front name from Houdini, the handcuff king, when Houdini saw him fall down a flight of stairs.

Gladys Leslie is to return to the silver sheet, playing opposite Lionel Barrymore in a forthcoming production.

For the sake of art Bull Montana is to be called Jack Montana after this. He was "Ferre, the Ape Man" in "Go and Get It" and his right name is Luigi Montagni.

"Forfaiture," the first grand opera adapted from a movie, has been given its premiere in Paris. It was adapted from "The Cheat," directed by Cecil DeMille with Fanny Ward as the star in 1915.

Sketch of the author Anzia Yezierska accompanying an article in the Cedar Rapids Evening Gazette, March 5th, 1921. Cedar Rapids Evening Gazette, March 5th, 1921. Uploaded by Kenmayer

Conclusion

Between 1880 and 1920 almost one and a half million immigrants found a new home in New York. By 1910 "41 percent of all New Yorkers were foreign born" (Foner, 2000, p.1). The culture and habits of New York were deeply influenced and in many cases shaped by the new arrivals. Politics, institutions, the way of living or the food changed throughout this process of immigration. A large number of the city's contemporary population descends from the immigrants of the 19th and early 20th century who were mainly Jews from Eastern Europe or immigrants from South Italy.

Today, the new wave of immigrants is mostly coming from the other continents of this planet. New arrivals from China, Mexico, the Dominican Republic or Jamaica add themselves to the already colorful face of the city. The Latin Americans, West Indies and Asians are dominating the current immigration stream, and by now more than a third of New York's inhabitants are immigrants.

The first masses of immigration entered the New World through the gates and halls of Ellis Island. Between 1892 and 1954 more than twelve million newcomers went through the inspection of this immigration port. Today the new arrivals mostly come through the gates of John F. Kennedy International Airport which is a much more comfortable way of travelling than in the old days.

Immigrants deeply affect the life and appearance of the city: multicultural neighborhoods, schools, restaurants, religious institutions and shops shape the face of New York. When the first immigration waves arrived almost 200 years ago the native-born Americans often regarded this process with fear and animosity. They were afraid to lose their dominant status and thought that the city might turn into a chaotic and lawless slum full of diseases, corruption and crime. They believed immigrants might take away their jobs and the prospering city might turn into an oversized almshouse.

Today those early immigrants are glorified and celebrated in museums, books, films, and stories. The new arrivals of today try to imitate their way. Certain images of the first immigrants are present in the cultural memory of today which remembers them as hard-working people who made every effort to find their way out of the gutter with their own bare hands or brains and who longed for assimilation. And still they had deeply rooted values, family bonds, traditions and customs. They were the very source that turned America into the great nation it is today. Nowadays, the nation is often afraid of the present immigrants who might alienate the country with their non-western background.

"New York is the quintessential immigrant city and has long been a main gateway for new arrivals" (Foner, 2000, p.5). Irish and Germans arrived in masses since the middle of the 19th century until the Eastern European Jews and the Italian immigrants took their place at the end of the 1800s. The Russian or Eastern European Jews and the Italians dominated the immigrant population of New York since then. However, they faced a lot of prejudices and discrimination.

Today many immigrants also work in sweatshops or own typical stores where they sell goods from their home country to keep some patriotism, traditions, habits and nostalgia alive. They as well as their predecessors often have the same reasons to come to America: Religious and political persecution, hunger, poverty, growing population, over-competition, overcrowding and discrimination in the home country, being expelled from countries and cities or forced to live in ghettos between two different nations where one has no national identity at all, anti-Semitic violence, being unwanted, unprotected and having little hope, as well as "chain migration, and the globalization of capitalism" brought masses of people to the United States.

The early immigrants arrived dirty, tired and hungry at Ellis Island. America promised to be the "golden land" where religious, political, social, academic, professional and educational freedom and opportunities were given and guaranteed.

For many Jewish immigrants the United States were finally a land were they could be free. After the first newcomers had arrived, masses followed. In Italy immigration to America was like a fever and became an epidemic. Returning emigrants were entitled "americanos", a name which included a success-story inconceivable to the people in the Old World. Going to America became so popular that it turned into the dream of every young Italian. Stories were told about the land where everything was possible and many people were inspired by the simple thought of this nation. This was not only true among the Italians, but among all the immigrants who came to the Promised Land. They had all heard of the American myth, the earthly paradise on the other side of the world, and this pulled them to the shores of this new continent in huge numbers.

New York is the entrance hall to the United States, it is the place where the new arrivals learn what it means to be an American. Today every fifth inhabitant of the megalopolis with its eight million people is a foreign-born immigrant.

Since the huge immigration wave from 1900 until 1910 there has never been such an enormous stream of newcomers until the 1990s when immigrants from 170 different countries arrived in New York. Almost five percent of New York State's population is Asian, which makes them the most rapidly growing group of immigrants.

With the building of the World Trade Center (WTC) the financial system of the world became more cosmopolitan, united under the roof of the Twin Towers. In the 1980s the face of the employees in the WTC began to change and now arrivals came from all over the world. Among the 79 employees of the restaurant "Windows on the World" there were immigrants from 13 different countries. An immigration wave had started again which was definitely comparable to the huge immigration waves of the 19th century. In the 1990s the WTC resembled a miniature edition of the United Nations.

When Giuliani was mayor of New York, delinquency could be cut drastically and New York became the safest metropolis of the United States. Besides, the city presented itself as a perfect example for social and economic opportunities of a complex and multicultural society. Already during the last decades of the 20th century New York inhabited an endlessly colorful mosaic of all nationalities, religions, skin colors and ethnicities. 186 different languages were spoken within the city. A moving evidence of extraordinary multiculturalism in New York's everyday life is the simple fact that the victims of 9/11 came from 93 different countries.

On the one hand New York is the most American city of all since it reflects the American way of life and the American Dream in its purest way. The capitalistic, fast moving, vivid, prosperous and colorful image of the city mirrors ideals and modern fairytales like "making it", "freedom", "from rags to riches", "pursuit of happiness, success and wealth" "independence" or "being unique". When the World Trade

Center collapsed in 2001 patriotism was the most significant reaction.

On the other hand New York is the most un-American of all cities since it can be described as one of the most international metropolises in the world. New York is an accumulation of all kinds of nations, cultures, ethnicities and religions. The whole world has found an accommodation in this unique microcosm.

Events that shake New York shake the whole world at the same time. A crash of the New York stock market has a deep impact on the world's economy and when the Twin Towers of the WTC were destroyed this was understood as an offense against the whole Western civilization, against democracy and Western values. Besides, inhabitants of New York are usually so proud of their city that they insist on being called New Yorkers instead of "just" being Americans.

The city's face changes every year with the income of all imaginable kinds of new arrivals and with the movement of the immigrants within the city. No matter if they live within their own districts, share multicultural quarters with dozens of other cultures and nations, or if they have spread separately all over the city, the immigrants now and then have and had an enormous and tremendous influence and impact on New York's character, culture, life style, outer appearance, and soul.

Assimilated or separated they present the city with a various amount of cultural, economic and social contributions. The vivid, colorful and multifaceted image of New York which fascinates and attracts millions of people every day would not exist if the rainbow-colored influx of immigrants had not taken place.

New York City is to a certain extent defined by the people who live there, and most of them have their ancestral roots abroad. And even though one cannot clearly conclude if the city is a melting pot or a salad bowl, since both definitions are true at the same time, this does not change the impressive picture New York leaves in the mind of its inhabitants as well as its visitors.

In fact the mixture of assimilated and separated characters on the metropolis' stage turns the daily performance of life in the city into a much more exciting occurrence.

Above:
The Immigrants, a bronze sculpture by Luis Sanguino (b.1934), located in Battery Park in New York City. Commissioned by Samuel Rudin as a memorial to his parents who immigrated to the United States in the late-19th century. Photographed in 2012 by 7mike5000

Below:
Montage of photographs, drawings and etchings by Jerome Myers depicting scenes of New York City from 1900-1935. Subject matter is largely of the lower East Side and the life of the new immigrants coming to America and the world they found here and the neighborhoods they created. Published in 1940. BEDownes. PD-Myers Photo Estate Collection.

American WWI poster. 1917. Text : "Remember Your First Thrill of AMERICAN
LIBERTY. YOUR DUTY - Buy United States Government Bonds 2nd Liberty
Loan of 1917." US-Library Of Congress.
U.S. National Archives and Records Administration

Bibliography

1) Besel, Uli and Kulgemeyer, Uwe. <u>Fräulein Freiheit. Miss Liberty Enlightening the World.</u> Transit Buchverlag: Berlin. 1986.

2) Bosse, Katharina and Butta, Carmen. <u>Strasse der Nationen</u>. p.132-152 . In GEO Special Nr.5. Gruner + Jahr AG & Co: Hamburg. October 1999.

3) Brownstone, David M.; Franck, Irene M; Brownstone, Douglass L. <u>Island of Hope, Island of Tears.</u> Rawson, Wade Publishers, Inc.: New York. 1979.

4) Burns, Ric; Sanders, James; and Ades, Lisa. <u>New York. Die Illustrierte Geschichte von 1609 bis Heute.</u> GEO and Frederking & Thaler Verlag GmbH: Munich. 2002.

5) Cahan, Abraham. <u>The Rise of David Levinsky</u> [1917]. Harper Torchbooks: New York, Hagerstown, San Francisco, London. 1966.

6) Cahan, Abraham. <u>Yekl</u> [1896] <u>and the Imported Bridegroom and other stories of the New York Ghetto</u> [1898]. Dover Publications, Inc.: New York. 1970.

7) Dos Passos, John. <u>Manhattan Transfer</u> [1925]. Houghton Mifflin Company: Boston. 1953.

8) Foner, Nancy. <u>From Ellis Island to JFK. New York's Two Great Waves of Immigration.</u> Yale University Press: New Haven and London; Russell Sage Foundation: New York. 2000.

9) Hamblin, B. Colin. Ellis Island. The Official Souvenir Guide. ARAMARK Sports and Entertainment Services, Inc. and Companion Press: Santa Barbara, California. 1994.

10) Higham, John. Send These to Me. Immigrants in Urban America. The Johns Hopkins University Press: Baltimore and London. 1984.

11) Homberger, Eric. The Historical Atlas of New York City: A Visual Celebration of Nearly 400 Years of New York City's History. An Owl Book. Henry Holt and Company: New York. 1998.

12) Lang, Barbara. The Process of Immigration in German-American Literature from 1850 to 1900. A Change in Ethnic Self-Definition. American Studies. A Monograph Series. Vol.64. Wilhelm Fink Verlag: Munich. 1988.

13) Riis, Jacob A. How the Other Half Lives [1890]. Dover Publications, Inc.: New York. 1971.

14) Weinberg, Sydney Stahl. The World of Our Mothers. The Lives of Jewish Immigrant Women. Schocken Books: New York. 1988.

15) Yezierska, Anzia. Bread Givers [1925]. Persea Books: New York.1975.

16) Yezierska, Anzia. How I Found America. Collected Stories of Anzia Yezierska. Persea Books: New York. 1991.

17) Yezierska, Anzia. Hungry Hearts and Other Stories [1920]. Persea Books: New York. 1991.

18) Yezierska, Anzia. <u>Red Ribbon on a White Horse</u>
[1950]. Persea Books: New York. 1987.

19) Yezierska, Anzia. <u>Salome of the Tenements </u>[1923].
University of Illinois Press: Urbana and Chicago. 1995.

About the Author

Eva Kolb was born in 1979 in Heidelberg (Germany). In Mannheim (Germany) she went to university and received her Bachelor of Arts degree in English, German, Film and Practical Media. During her studies she worked in film companies in New York (USA) and Paris (France). Apart from living in New York, she also studied the city and its history in university. In 2005 she moved to Munich (Germany) to work as an editor, teacher and writer. With this book the authoress combines her fascination for history as well as her love for the city of New York.

This book is a new edition of the book "The Evolution of New York City's Multiculturalism: Melting Pot or Salad Bowl: Immigrants in New York from the 19th Century until the End of the Gilded Age".

© Text by Eva Kolb & Textwerkstatt München
All rights reserved.

Images taken from Wikimedia Commons

Published in Munich, August 2014

Herstellung und Verlag:
BoD – Books on Demand, Norderstedt
ISBN 9783735777904